The outrageous book of bizarre choices

The outrageous book of bizarre choices

**Created by Randy Horn
with Darcy Horn**

WORKMAN PUBLISHING • NEW YORK

Written by Randy Horn, Darcy Horn,
Jess Brallier, and Sally Chabert

Library of Congress Cataloging-in-Publication Data
Horn, Randy.
Zobmondo!! : the outrageous book of bizarre choices / created by
Randy Horn with Darcy Horn.
p. cm.
ISBN-13: 978-0-7611-2420-7 (alk. paper)
ISBN-10: 0-7611-2420-9 (alk. paper)
1. Curiosities and wonders—Humor. I. Horn, Darcy. II. Title
PN6231.C85 H67 2001
818'.5402—DC21   2001026988

Workman books are available at discounts when purchased
in bulk for premiums and sales promotions as well as for
fund-raising or educational use. Special editions or
book excerpts can also be created to specification. For details,
contact the Special Sales Director at the address below.

Workman Publishing Company, Inc.
225 Varick Street
New York, NY 10014-4381
www.workman.com

Printed in U.S.A.

First printing October 2001

15 14 13 12 11 10

Welcome to Our Twisted World of Bizarre Choices

You are about to experience the world's most exciting collection of questions and trivia. But first, a definition:

Zobmondo!! *(zob-MAHN-doe)* is a slang expression derived from the negative exclamation "zob," to express horror, pain, or frustration: *"Mary tripped over the log and stubbed her toe. 'Zob!' she cried."* Zobmondo!! expresses the utter dismay that zob cannot begin to describe:

"*As Mary broke her foot and looked down to see the bone protruding from the side of her shoe, she screamed in excruciating pain, 'Zobmondo!!'*" Within the context of this book, the word *Zobmondo!!* would likely be heard after a question is asked. The expression reflects the difficulty that one faces in choosing between the equally unappealing and often horrific options in each question.

Zobmondo!'s purpose is to inspire ridiculous, fun conversation and debate. *Zobmondo!!* (the book) is comprised of wild questions that ask you to choose between the two options provided. Questions can be used alone or with friends—even as a party game. We recommend that you choose your answer and then justify and defend it to the death. Therein lies the real humor of *Zobmondo!!* and therein lie the insights and windows into the twisted minds of your friends and family.

In addition, each question comes with trivia or jokes meant to enlighten you, to enrich debate, to amuse those waiting for a person's decision, or to mentally file away for later use when you're trying to impress attractive people.

Zobmondo!!'s additional rules:

1. Abstinence is strictly forbidden in *Zobmondo!!* The phrases "I won't choose either," "Neither one," "Who cares?" and/or "I would rather die" should never be uttered while discussing a *Zobmondo!!* question.

2. No condiments, plastic surgery, or actions that change the spirit of the question may be added to a *Zobmondo!!* scenario. The bottom line is you must assume that you are forced to choose between the two options of each "dilemma of unenjoyment" *as it is presented;* you may not explain away the question by

drowning everything in ketchup or resolving to have the ugly growth removed with plastic surgery.

3. The jokes and trivia provided may not be used as a diversionary tactic to avoid making choices.

And whatever you do, do not try to digest the contents of this book in one sitting. Not only will you become nauseated and go completely numb with horrendous images, but more important, you will not be able to appreciate the crazy social dynamic that is created by spontaneously discussing these questions *in moderation* with your friends and acquaintances.

Zobmondo!! disclaimer: While some of these questions may paint a violent, risqué, shocking, nauseating, perplexing, sickening, or downright disturbing picture . . . they are not to be taken literally or meant to offend. Take them with a grain of salt. They are designed to make you think and engage in a lively discussion. Feel free to skip questions that are too vivid for your particular audience. But regardless of your choices, please place yourself in the proper fun, social state of mind before discussing a *Zobmondo!!* question.

Bear in mind that the authors of this book and the crazy board game it was based on have not performed any of these stunts, and we *strongly* advise you to refrain from trying any actions described on the following pages. Neither the authors of this book nor its publisher shall be liable for any damage that may be caused or sustained as a result of conducting any of the activities in this book.

Welcome to the world of *Zobmondo!!*

Zobmondo!! warning:

Proceed with caution.
This book is only for those with
a twisted imagination. Be prepared to leave
conventional thought behind and
join the ranks of the demented and insane.

Chew on a wild rat's severed tail for a half hour

OR

thoroughly brush your teeth with a toothbrush from a prison's community toothbrush bowl?

In the 1300s, rats carrying deadly fleas—on their tails, behind their ears, all over!—brought the Black Plague to Europe, killing two-thirds of the continent's population.

THE TOOTHBRUSH WAS INVENTED IN PRISON. IN 1770, LONDON PRISONER WILLIAM ADDIS ATTACHED SOME BRISTLES TO A BONE AND INVENTED THE TOOTHBRUSH. WHEN RELEASED, HE STARTED A TOOTHBRUSH BUSINESS THAT WAS IMMEDIATELY SUCCESSFUL. ATTA BOY, WILLIAM!

Bite into a piece of chocolate and find it filled with maggots

OR

filled with pus?

Chocolate has been around since the Mayans had their heyday in South America. They called it the food of the gods. The Spanish took it back to Europe. At one point there were so many chocolate houses in England that they threatened the existence of the traditional English pub! Until the late 1800s, chocolate was consumed as a drink, and that was only for wealthy males— it was considered unhealthy for women and children.

SINCE 1995 THERE HAS BEEN A 400% INCREASE IN THE NUMBER OF SURGEONS WORLDWIDE WHO CLEANSE WOUNDS WITH MAGGOTS.

Pus is made up of a thin liquid called *liquer puris*, plus the white cells—called leukocytes— that your body uses to clean its wounds. Certain leukocytes, known as bacteriophages, eat the bacteria in the wound.

Walk around all day with a dead mouse in your butt

OR

a dead frog in your mouth?

In Cleveland, Ohio, it is illegal to kill mice without a hunting license. (But there's nothing on the books about catching them with your butt.)

A GROUP OF MICE IS CALLED A NEST. A GROUP OF FROGS IS CALLED AN ARMY.

Exterminators say: If you see one mouse in your house, you probably have a dozen. The same ratio does not apply to seeing a dead mouse in your butt or a dead frog in your mouth.

Be constantly depressed

OR

constantly afraid?

"HE'S TURNED HIS LIFE
AROUND. HE USED
TO BE DEPRESSED
AND MISERABLE.
NOW HE'S MISERABLE
AND DEPRESSED."
—David Frost

"Everyone has some fear. A man who has
no fear belongs in a mental institution.
Or on special teams."
—WALT MICHAELS, FORMER NEW YORK JETS COACH

Be accused of discriminating against someone because of age

OR

gender?

ON AVERAGE, PLAINTIFFS WHO WIN DISCRIMINATION SUITS IN THE U.S. ARE AWARDED OVER $250,000 IN COMPENSATORY DAMAGES.

In 1984, after blaming slow mail delivery on "all those stupid broads we have working in the Post Office now," Clarence Duffy, of the Dubuque, Iowa, Human Rights Commission, resigned his post.

Have a Texas accent and live in New York City

OR

have a New York accent and live in Texas?

IN 1997 THE RATIO OF NEW YORKERS BITTEN BY RATS TO THE NUMBER BITTEN BY OTHER NEW YORKERS WAS 1:7.

Dallas has more tanning salons than any other city in the U.S.

"THAT LOWDOWN SCOUNDREL DESERVES TO BE KICKED TO DEATH BY A JACKASS, AND I'M JUST THE ONE TO DO IT."

—A congressional candidate in Texas

There were 240 pedestrian fatalities in New York City in 1994.

Have the CIA after you

OR

have the Mafia after you?

"By then, Gold had learned in Washington
that the CIA was recruiting mercenaries to
fight in Africa. He learned this at breakfast
from his morning paper when he read:

CIA DENIES RECRUITING MERCENARIES TO FIGHT IN AFRICA."

—JOSEPH HELLER, *GOOD AS GOLD*

"Organized crime in America takes in
over forty billion dollars a year and spends
very little on office supplies."

—WOODY ALLEN

As a man, live with a permanent eight-inch erection

OR

a two-inch penis?

IF YOU'RE GOING TO HAVE A LIFELONG ERECTION, IT'S TOO BAD YOU'RE STUCK WITH THE HUMAN PENIS—IT'S SO BORING! THE PIG'S PENIS HAS A CORKSCREW TIP; THE RHINO'S IS TWO FEET LONG; AND THE PORCUPINE'S, WHEN ERECT, CAN SHOOT A SEVEN-FOOT STREAM OF PEE. (IMAGINE IF GENETIC CLONING ENGINEERS COMBINED ALL THESE PENILE TRAITS INTO THE WORLD'S GREATEST PENIS. IT'D BE THE SWISS ARMY KNIFE OF PENISES.)

The smallest erect human penis on record was one centimeter long.

Eat all your food
liquefied and frozen,
like a Popsicle

OR

have strangers squish
all your food like wine grapes
with their perfectly clean
but bare feet before you eat it?

FDR's favorite food:
fried cornmeal mush

President Eisenhower's:
prune whip

Make your living by manufacturing sex toys

OR

guns?

IN 1996 THE RATIO OF HANDGUN MURDERS PER CAPITA IN CANADA TO HANDGUN MURDERS PER CAPITA IN AMERICA WAS 1 TO 324. THE SEX TOY MURDER RATE WAS UNAVAILABLE AT PRESS TIME.

Fall through the toilet hole in an outhouse

OR

be temporarily trapped beneath a pile of dead animals?

IVANHOE, VA, August 18, 2000—For three days, Coolidge Winesett sat mired in the five-foot-deep hole of a partially collapsed outhouse, alternately yelling for help and trying to cope with the stench.

"I tell you what, it was hard to get one breath down there," said Winesett, age 75.

Winesett was rescued by a mail carrier who noticed that Winesett's deliveries were still in the box. Jimmy Jackson, the mail carrier, found no sign of Winesett at his house or car. But Jackson spotted Winesett's crutch propped beside the outhouse. "The closer I got, I heard a faint sound like somebody trying to holler," Jackson said.

Winesett fell when the outhouse floor and part of a wall gave way. "Down it went and took me with it," he said. "I thought it was an earthquake. Then I realized where I was at. I done a lot of hollering, but nobody couldn't hear me."

The collapsed floor saved Winesett from being dunked in the deepest sludge. He was hospitalized for dehydration and infection from the scratches.

Joe Kulis of Bedford, Ohio, is one of many in the business of freeze-drying dead pets. (The "sleep" pose is cheapest; a large dog in "attack" pose is much more expensive.) Your dead pet can be sent to Joe by Federal Express, Air Freight, or—get a load of this—Greyhound.

Have to spend an entire pro basketball game with your face sticking right above the rim

OR

an entire hockey game with your face sticking out into the middle of the goal net?

232 shots (many of them "slams" delivered by 280-pound seven-footers) hit the basket in an average NBA game.

"My biggest thrill came the night Elgin Baylor and I combined for 73 points in Madison Square Garden. Elgin had 71 of them."

—HOT ROD HUNDLEY

"A HARD RUBBER DISK THAT HOCKEY PLAYERS STRIKE WHEN THEY CAN'T HIT ONE ANOTHER."

—sportswriter Jimmy Cannon, on what a puck is

There are 40 shots (many traveling at over 100 miles per hour) on net per NHL match.

Chew a mole off someone's neck

OR

drink a half cup of your best friend's blood?

A mole is a nevus, which is lots of melanin-packed cells all bunched together. Melanin is what gives your skin color.

IN AFRICA, THE MASAI MAKE "BLOODSHAKES" BY INSERTING A STRAW INTO THE NECK OF A LIVING ANIMAL AND SUCKING OUT THE BLOOD.

Show up noticeably drunk on a national TV show

OR

roaring drunk at your child's college graduation?

At any one time, 0.7% of Americans are drunk.

And odds are 1 in 4 that any one American has appeared on TV.

So what are the chances of you showing up drunk on TV? You do the math. (We can't, we're hungover. Got drunk on *Real World*.)

At a 1985 dinner, Washington Redskins fullback John Riggins told Supreme Court justice Sandra Day O'Connor, "Come on, Sandy, baby, loosen up. You're too tight." Then he passed out on the floor.

Have to dangle from a
1,000-foot cliff on a rope
tied to a tree and choose
to tie the knot yourself

OR

trust an Eagle Scout
with a knot-tying merit badge
to tie it?

"WHEN YOU GET TO THE
END OF YOUR ROPE, TIE
A KNOT AND HANG ON."
—Franklin D. Roosevelt

THE BOY SCOUT HANDBOOK
(EIGHTH EDITION) CLAIMS
THAT "THE BOWLINE IS THE
BEST KNOT FOR FORMING
A LOOP THAT WON'T SLIP."

Always have to write
with your
nondominant hand

OR

always have to write
with your
eyes closed?

Right-handed people live,
on average, nine years
longer than left-handed
people do.

MORE THAN 2,500 LEFT-HANDED
PEOPLE DIE EVERY YEAR FROM
USING RIGHT-HANDED PRODUCTS.

Be trapped in jail with a guard who hates you

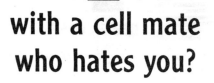

OR

with a cell mate who hates you?

TOP TEN PRISON FLICKS

10. *Ernest Goes to Jail*
9. *The Green Mile*
8. *Women in Cell Block 7*
7. *The Great Escape*
6. *Birdman of Alcatraz*
5. *Slammer Girls*
4. *Ilsa, the Wicked Warden*
3. *Papillon*
2. *The Shawshank Redemption*
1. *Cool Hand Luke*

WOULD YOU RATHER...

As a lumberjack 100 feet up a large tree, suddenly come upon a hive of bees

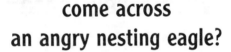

OR

come across an angry nesting eagle?

A BEE FACT (not good for lumberjacks): The average bee hive has up to 120,000 bees (each with a stinger). That's a lot, at any height.

A BEE FACT (interesting, but not the least bit helpful to lumberjacks): More people are killed by bees every year than by sharks.

AN EAGLE FACT: Al Gore received a letter from a Texas couple complaining that the Clinton administration was slashing funding for programs, which would endanger the Texas Eagle. Al Gore wrote back, sharing his concern with the couple and assuring them that he had always fought, and would continue to fight, to save endangered species.

Oops. The Texas Eagle is not a bird. It is an airplane shuttle that runs to Illinois. The couple used it to visit their grandchildren.

AN EAGLE FACT (of no value to lumberjacks but really quite amazing): Eagles have sex while cruising at up to 60 mph in flight. And it's not unusual for both eagles to slam into the ground before they finish. Wow! Talk about a climax!

Get a bad case of poison ivy way up inside your nose

OR

inside your inner ear?

It doesn't matter! Because the Electronic Itch Stopper is now available from the HonTech Foundation for Medical Technology at Post Office Box 400956 in Cambridge, MA 02138, or at www.ItchStopper.com.

Slide down a 1,000-foot rope with every part of your body covered except your hands

do the same thing wearing only gloves and shorts?

OR do what some guy in Placer County, California, did? He swung off the 728-foot-high Foresthill Bridge, tied to a 115-foot rope. That part was OK. But when he tried to climb the rope back to the bridge, ice crystals had formed on the rope, preventing his climb. He hung for more than three hours in the frigid morning air until rescuers arrived and hauled him up.

Give birth to a child
knowing there is a 25% chance
you'll die during childbirth

OR

never have children
of your own at all?

"HAVING CHILDREN
IS LIKE HAVING A
BOWLING ALLEY
INSTALLED IN YOUR
BRAIN."
—Martin Mull

Louisa May
Alcott, author
of the classic
Little Women,
hated children.
She only wrote
the book because
her publisher
asked her to.

While trying to fight off
a polar bear,
be armed with a stun gun

OR

a spear?

**A GROUP
OF BEARS IS
KNOWN AS
A SLOTH.**

A big polar bear and a little rabbit are
taking a dump side by side in the snow.
The bear looks down at the rabbit and in
a deep voice says, "Excuse me, Mr. Rabbit,
but do you have trouble with poop sticking
to your fur?"

The rabbit looks up at the huge bear
and in his squeaky voice says, "Why, no,
Mr. Bear. I sure do not."

So the bear scoops up the rabbit and
wipes his butt with him.

A polar bear's skin is black. The fur of its coat is about 1.2
inches long. Its dense, woolly, insulating layer of
underhair is covered by a relatively thin layer of stiff,
shiny, clear guard hairs. The fur is oily and water
repellent and can be white, creamy yellow, or brown.
Polar bears molt (shed and replace their fur) annually,
in May or June. The molt can last several weeks.

Walk around from now on wearing shoes with little suction cups

OR

metal cleats on the bottom?

THE FOOTPADS OF GECKOS ARE COVERED IN THOUSANDS OF FIBERS, EACH WITH A SUCTION CUP AT THE END. THIS IS WHY THEY CAN WALK UPSIDE DOWN.

When astronauts landed on the moon, they wore boots with Velcro hooks on the bottom, and the steps of the ladder that went from the lunar module to the moon were covered with Velcro loops. So it was Velcro—not mushy suction cups or clumsy metal cleats—that kept Neil Armstrong from falling at that most historic of moments.

Be accidentally hit in the head very hard with a sock with a potato in it

OR

with a rubber hose?

BANGING YOUR HEAD AGAINST A WALL USES **150** CALORIES AN HOUR. BANGING YOUR HEAD WITH A SOCKED POTATO OUGHT TO DO THE SAME.

"UP YOUR NOSE WITH A RUBBER HOSE."

—Vinnie Barbarino, *Welcome Back, Kotter*

Two German motorists had an all-too-literal head-on collision near the small town of Gütersloh. The two were coming from opposite directions, carefully steering their cars down the center of the road through dense fog. At the moment of impact, each had his head craned out of the driver-side window. Their noggins slammed each other and both men were hospitalized with severe head injuries. Their cars weren't scratched.

Die before your spouse of fifty years does, knowing he or she will be healthy but heartbroken for another twenty years

OR

watch your spouse die before you after fifty years together?

A man from Maine heads to Florida for a weekend trip; his wife is coming to meet him the next day. He gets to his room, sets up his laptop computer, and sends her a short e-mail to let her know he has arrived. Unfortunately, he makes a typo in the address and his note is sent to the elderly wife of a minister who just died. When the grieving widow checks her e-mail later that day, she lets out a scream and falls to the floor. Her children come rushing in to find the following on her screen:

Dearest Wife,

I have just arrived. Everything is prepared for your arrival tomorrow. Can't wait to see you.

Your Loving Husband

P.S.: It sure is hot down here!

Stick your hand into a sealed box of rattlesnakes

OR

stick your hand into a box filled with unknown contents that are making a mechanical buzzing sound?

The Consumer Product Safety Review found that in 1998:

1. 107,385 people were injured by manual tools
2. 53,411 people were injured by lawn and garden equipment
3. 32,030 people were injured by home power tools (excluding saws)
4. 29,684 people were injured by chainsaws

A rattlesnake's venom is less potent than a black widow spider's.

Have regular encounters with aliens and not have any proof

OR

have your best friend be invisible?

Jimmy Carter was the first president of the United States to see (or, at least, admit to seeing) a UFO. In 1969, Carter and a few buddies saw a multicolored saucer moving across the evening sky. "It seemed to move toward us from a distance," Carter noted, "then it stopped and moved partially away. It returned and departed. It came close . . . maybe three hundred to one thousand yards away . . . moved away, came close, and then moved away." (And they say it was Billy who had the drinking problem.)

"And this, this is, this is the most interesting thing about the whole thing—he said 'What a coincidence. My name happens to be Harvey.'"

—JIMMY STEWART, ABOUT AN INVISIBLE RABBIT HE HAS BEFRIENDED IN THE FILM *HARVEY* (1950)

Be dating someone who insists
that every electric device
in both of your homes
be controlled by those
"clap on, clap off" devices

OR

that every piece of furniture
have plastic covers?

SEARCH THE INTERNET AND YOU'LL
EVENTUALLY DISCOVER THAT THE SAME
COMPANY THAT BROUGHT US THE
CLAPPER® ALSO BROUGHT US THE
CHIA PET®. NOW THERE'S A STUNNING
COINCIDENCE.

Have every driver but you be a "student driver"

OR

have every driver (except you) on the road be at least 75 years old?

On April 29, 1970, Mrs. Miriam Hargrave crashed through a set of red lights and failed her driving test for the 39th time. She vowed to try again in four months.

AGE AT WHICH, STATISTICALLY, OLDER MALE DRIVERS BECOME A MENACE TO THEMSELVES AND OTHER MOTORISTS: **71**

"Have you ever noticed that anybody going slower than you is an idiot, and anyone going faster than you is a maniac?"

—GEORGE CARLIN

AGE AT WHICH THE AVERAGE GUY FINALLY HANGS UP HIS CAR KEYS: **85**

Marry your first boyfriend/girlfriend

OR

marry someone your parents chose for you?

JOHN LENNON'S FIRST GIRLFRIEND WAS
NAMED THELMA PICKLES. WHICH EXPLAINS WHY
LENNON WAS THE ONE GUY WHO THOUGHT
"YOKO ONO" WAS A PERFECTLY FINE NAME.

Meanwhile, at age 47, the Rolling Stones'
Bill Wyman began a relationship with
13-year-old Mandy Smith. The affair had
the blessing of Mandy's mother. Six years
later, Bill and Mandy married, but the
marriage only lasted a year.

Not long after, Bill's 30-year-old son
Stephen married Mandy's mother, age 46.
That made Stephen a stepfather to his
former stepmother.

If Bill and Mandy had remained married,
Stephen would have been his father's father-
in-law and his own grandpa.

Take a bumpy two-mile ride
sitting wedged
(feet hanging out) in
the main compartment of
a small metal shopping cart

OR

take a 25-mile ride
in the empty but rotating bin
of a cement truck?

If one guy leaves Nashville for Tallahassee at noon in a shopping cart traveling 8 miles per hour, and at midnight another guy leaves Tallahassee headed for Nashville in the bin of a cement truck traveling 45 miles per hour, who will be closer to Nashville when they meet?

Neither will be closer. They'll be at the same point when they "meet."

Have your thumb and first finger glued together for life in the "OK" sign

OR

be forced to say "thank you" before every sentence?

THANK YOU, BUT BE CAREFUL.

THANK YOU, FOR IN BRAZIL, RUSSIA, AND GREECE, THE THUMB-AND-FINGER "OK" SIGN IS OBSCENE.

THANK YOU, BECAUSE YOU DON'T WANT TO BE GETTING BEAT UP ALL OVER THE WORLD.

THANK YOU.

Always have to wear wet socks

OR

always have to wear wet underwear?

It's only because of dikes, canals, and pumps that the lower-than-sea-level Netherlands isn't constantly flooded. But the land's still soggy, and the Dutch got tired of wearing wet socks long before rubber shoes started showing up. Which is why they came up with water-resistant wooden shoes.

Always spit when you talk

OR

always be spit on when spoken to?

IT DEPENDS . . .

For the Masai people of Tanzania, Africa, spitting is considered a show of goodwill. Newborn babies are spat upon to bring the child luck, and deals are often closed only after the traders spit upon one another.

Be granted the answers to any three questions

OR

be granted the ability to resurrect one person?

SAMPLE QUESTIONS

Why don't sheep shrink in the rain?

Why do men have nipples?

How does the guy who drives the morning snowplow get to work?

How does an astronaut go to the bathroom?

Why do we drive on parkways and park on driveways?

Did Adam and Eve have belly buttons?

How much deeper would the ocean be if all those sponges didn't live there soaking up water?

Who shot JFK?

SAMPLE PEOPLE

John Candy

John Belushi

Rock Hudson

Princess Di

The Virgin Mary

Chris Farley

Marilyn Monroe

Abraham Lincoln

Jesus

Elvis

Be confronted on the street by a loud, angry panhandler for a week straight

by an unbearably persistent Bible thumper?

What is the biggest problem for an atheist?
No one to talk to during an orgasm.

THE BIBLE IS THE MOST SHOPLIFTED BOOK IN THE UNITED STATES.

In a fight, be armed with an eight-inch knife

OR

a crowbar?

In November 2000, Paul Cheatham, 61, of Illinois was out for a walk when a deer jumped him. Cheatham grabbed the six-point, 130-pound buck by the horns, held it with one hand, opened a pocketknife with his mouth, and jabbed the deer in the rib cage until it was dead. "I hung on and got my legs around his neck," Cheatham said, "and we wrestled around quite a while." Cheatham suffered bruises over much of his body.

Have to go to the bathroom in a giant cat-litter box inside your house

OR

anywhere you want, but only outside?

In 1991, the Scott Paper Company did a survey to find out about people's bathroom habits. Here are two highlights:

1. You can guess people's education by whether they read in the bathroom: 67% of people with master's degrees or higher read on the can, compared with 56% of people with college degrees and 50% of those with high school diplomas.

2. 55% of Americans fold their toilet tissue neatly, while 35% wad it up before using it.

Spend a week at school in your underwear

OR

attend two classes completely nude?

The following are written excuses given to teachers in Albuquerque.

"My son is under the doctor's care and should not take fizical ed. Please execute him."

"Maryann was absent Dec. 11–16, because she had a fever, sore throat, headache, and upset stomach. Her sister was also sick, fever and sore throat, her brother had a low-grade fever. There must be the flu going around, her father even got hot last night."

"Please excuse pedro from being absent yesterday. He had ~~Diah~~, ~~diahoah~~, ~~dyah~~, the sh!@s."

"I just don't feel that my algebra teacher should ever know what my butt looks like."

—ACTRESS JULIA ROBERTS ON WHY SHE WON'T DO NUDE SCENES

As a hitchhiker, see handcuffs and a chain saw in the back seat

OR

see bloody clothing in the back seat?

Visit www.urbanlegends.com and you'll discover that over 300 people have posted detailed messages about urban legends that involve a hitchhiker. So what's scarier—killer hitchhikers, or that 300 people out there have the need and time to debate one urban legend?

"NOW THEY SHOW YOU HOW DETERGENTS TAKE OUT BLOODSTAINS, A PRETTY VIOLENT IMAGE THERE. I THINK IF YOU'VE GOT A T-SHIRT WITH A BLOODSTAIN ALL OVER IT, MAYBE LAUNDRY ISN'T YOUR BIGGEST PROBLEM. MAYBE YOU SHOULD GET RID OF THE BODY BEFORE YOU DO THE WASH."

—Jerry Seinfeld

Always show up 20 minutes late for everything

OR

always show up 90 minutes early for everything?

VIDEO RECOMMENDATION TIME!

Sliding Doors (1998)

The sliding doors are those of a London subway train. If Helen (Gwyneth Paltrow) makes it through before they close, her life (and loves) go one way. If she's left on the platform, they go another. The audience watches what develops in both options. (Back and forth, from short blonde hair to long brown hair, and back again.) We're not even talking 20 or 90 minutes here— just a split second before one's life goes flying off with a cheating bum or a clever, caring, and likable sort.

ON AVERAGE, AMERICANS SPEND **33.24** MINUTES MAKING LOVE, INCLUDING FOREPLAY, PER SESSION. AND THE AVERAGE WOMAN SAYS SHE WOULD LIKE AN ADDITIONAL **12** MINUTES.

Eat one small hotel bar of soap

OR

six sticks of butter?

(Here's some great info for guys who love naked women.)

Woodbury Soap was the first product to show a nude woman in its advertisements. The year was 1936. Edward Steichen's photograph showed a rear, full-length view of a woman sunbathing—wearing only sandals.

AND IF YOU FOLD AN EMPTY ONE-POUND BOX OF LAND O'LAKES BUTTER JUST RIGHT, THE TWO KNEECAPS ON THE NATIVE AMERICAN WOMAN CAN BE MADE TO LOOK LIKE HER TWO BARE BREASTS. MOST PEOPLE CAN FIGURE IT OUT BY THE FOURTH ATTEMPT.

Bang your funny bone five times in a row until it's not funny anymore

OR

listen to somebody scrape nails down a chalkboard for 20 minutes?

THE REAL STORY BEHIND THE FUNNY BONE

The funny bone is actually the ulnar nerve, a long nerve that runs from the spinal cord in your back all the way down to your fingertips. At your elbow is the one place where there's no muscle or fat protecting it. Hit your elbow and the ulnar nerve slams against bone. OUCH!

A CLASSROOM JOKE

TEACHER: George, go to the map and find North America.

GEORGE: Here it is!

TEACHER : Correct. Now, class, who discovered America?

CLASS: George!

Eat your entire diet cold

OR

eat your entire diet overcooked?

"I LIKE MY OYSTERS FRIED.
THAT WAY I KNOW THEY'VE DIED."

—Roy Blount, Jr.

As a male in grade school, be known as a "momma's boy"

OR

a "brown noser"?

A funny grade school joke . . .

One day the first grade teacher was reading the story of the three little pigs to her class. She came to the part of the story where the first pig was trying to accumulate the building materials for his home. She read, ". . . And so the pig went up to the man with the wheelbarrow full of straw and said, 'Pardon me sir, but may I have some of that straw to build my house?'"

The teacher paused, then asked the class, "And what do you think that man said?"

One little boy raised his hand and said, "I think he said 'Holy sh@#! A talking pig!'"

Have to learn sword swallowing

OR

fire eating?

ROAD TRIP!

Head for the video section of Ripley's Believe It or Not! Museum on Fisherman's Wharf in San Francisco. Not only can you see sword swallowers and fire eaters, but also a four-eyed guy, the world's most kissed man, and people blowing smoke through their eyes. Phone ahead: (415) 771-6188.

Work for your sibling

OR

for your best friend?

A thorough review of assorted business listings confirms that there are thousands of business names ending with "and sons" and none with "and friends." There's got to be some good reason. The market's never wrong.

A survey of personnel directors of America's hundred largest companies cited these unusual employee interview experiences:

One applicant interrupted her interview to phone her therapist for advice on how to answer specific interview questions.

One applicant asked, "I know this is off the subject, but will you marry me?"

Meet your greatest hero and vomit on him or her

OR

in trying to meet him or her, be arrested and publicly accused of stalking?

President George H. W. Bush (a hero to many) went to Japan and, on international television, vomited all over the prime minister of Japan (a hero to many).

A couple of years later, over 600 young Japanese viewers of Pokémon (heroes to many) vomited like crazy when a scene from the cartoon series featured a bright red explosion that filled the TV screen.

MEANWHILE, THE LONGEST RECORDED DISTANCE FOR PROJECTILE VOMITING IS 27 FEET. (BET YA IT WAS SOMEBODY IN JAPAN. WHAT IS IT— ALL THAT RAW FISH?)

Be trapped in an elevator packed with wet dogs

three fat men with bad breath?

This guy's in the rear of a full hotel elevator and he shouts, "Ballroom, please."

A lady standing in front of him turns around and says, "I'm sorry, I didn't realize I was crowding you."

Have the brakes go out on your car on a hilltop

OR

have to go into a biker bar and yell "You guys are a bunch of pussies"?

Helpful Hints for Jumping from Your Brakeless Car
Use the emergency brake (it may slow down the car). Open the door and jump out. Now this is important: Jump so the car doesn't hit you. Remember, you're on the same trajectory as the car. You gotta jump out and back. Aim for something other than cement (bushes, leaves, grass). Pull in your head, legs, and arms and roll when you hit ground. Pray.

Helpful Hints for the Bikers Who Will Soon be Jumping on Your Car
Start with a great helmet and the best leather shoes, pants, and jacket that money can buy. Make sure you've got a long, straight stretch of road ahead. Pull the motorcycle alongside the car and make sure both are going the same speed. Get the bike as close to the car as possible. Stand crouched with both feet on the seat. Hold throttle until last second. Jump headfirst into a window. Pray.

Wake up to find a roach sucking on your tear duct for moisture

OR

find two rats having sex on your stomach?

ABOUT 20% OF ALL ADULTS IN THE U.S. HAVE HAD A COCKROACH CRAWL INTO THEIR INNER EAR CANAL. (THEY ENTER WHILE YOU SLEEP!)

PREGNANT FEMALE RATS GIVE BIRTH TO LITTERS THAT RANGE FROM SIX TO TWENTY-TWO BABIES. THOSE BABIES THEN BEGIN BREEDING WHEN THEY REACH FOUR MONTHS OF AGE.

Given that you are a 45-minute walk or 20-minute run from the nearest toilet facility and you have a strong need to take an immediate dump, walk

OR

run to the toilet?

Either way, you'd better pray that U.S. Patent #3,477,070 is not in use. That patent was awarded for a Toilet Lid Lock that prevents unauthorized access to the toilet bowl.

On the other hand, if the need is that strong, you might hope that U.S. Patent #3,593,345 is in use. That patent is for Whisper Seat, a toilet seat with an acoustical barrier that keeps other people from hearing really embarrassing sounds.

And then there's the Super Bowl 2000, a glow-in-the-dark toilet seat introduced in 1987. Its inventors projected that their seat would be a fixture "in every house in America by the year 2000." (Is it in yours?)

Be the boy in the plastic bubble

OR

the elephant man?

I think I would rather be either of these two than the guy that had to take dictation for President Johnson. Few presidents have permitted the kind of intimacy between themselves and their staffs that Johnson encouraged. When he had to go to the bathroom in the middle of a conversation, it was not unusual for him to move the discussion there. Johnson seemed delighted as he recounted the tale of "one of those delicate Kennedyites who came into the bathroom with me and then found it utterly impossible to look at me while I sat there on the toilet."

Be married to someone who is extremely vain

OR

has an extremely poor self-image?

"I think it's upsetting to people that Donald and I have it all: We're young, we're healthy, we love our work and we have a good marriage and children on top of that! People can't stand that."

—IVANA TRUMP

"I CAN'T BELIEVE I'M MARRIED. THIS IS THE PRIME TIME FOR ME."

—Donald Trump, on young women

Accidentally slam your hand down on a telephone message spike

OR

get just the tips of your fingers caught in a paper shredder?

OFFICIAL WARNING!
Child and Cat Alert!

If you have a paper shredder in a home environment where there are children or animals, it should be left unplugged. Children's fingers and cats (hey, this is documented) can get into a shredder. The shredders equipped with a photo-eye start are especially dangerous.

Note: No such warning has been issued for cats and telephone message spikes.

Eat a cooked beaver tail

OR

a cooked cow udder?

CALVES' EYES STUFFED WITH BREADCRUMBS
AND ROASTED ARE A POPULAR MEAL IN
ENGLAND, WHILE COW TESTICLES ARE
ENJOYED ALL OVER SOUTH AMERICA.
WATCH FOR UDDERS AS THE NEXT TREND.

FRICASSEED BEAVER TAIL

Skin the tail and cut it into serving pieces. Shake the pieces in
a plastic bag of ¼ cup flour, 1 teaspoon salt, 1 teaspoon freshly
ground pepper, and 1 teaspoon sage. Heat 6 tablespoons of
bacon fat in a skillet and brown the pieces on both sides over
rather high heat. When nicely colored, add 1½ cups of chicken
broth and reduce the heat. Simmer, covered, until tender
(45 minutes to an hour). Add ¼ cup bourbon.

While the stew's cooking, brown 12 small white onions in
butter, glaze with 2 tablespoons granulated sugar, and cook,
covered, over low heat until just tender. Arrange the meat on
a serving dish with the onions and the sauce, and garnish with
chopped parsley. Serve with hot dumplings and pear preserves.

Be left completely naked with no possessions in a foreign country

OR

in your place of work?

This is exactly why you should write on your body (in ink!) the following:
   AT&T international calling card number
   American Embassy phone number .
   American Express phone number
   American Express card number (and expiration date)

What possession do you think Sandy Hill Pittman brought with her on her 1996 climb up Mount Everest?

An espresso maker

THERE IS AT LEAST ONE TIME (WHICH WE KNOW OF) WHEN GERALDO RIVERA WAS COMPLETELY NAKED AT WORK. SERIOUSLY! IN 1989, THE "JOURNALIST" DID A SHOW, NAKED, FROM A NUDIST CAMP.

A first grade teacher collected well-known proverbs. He gave each kid in the class the first half of the proverb, and asked them to come up with the rest. Here is what a kid came up with:
   People in glass houses shouldn't . . .
   run around naked.

Walk the stairs to the top of the Sears Tower while carrying a 40-pound backpack

OR

with a large pebble in each shoe?

MINI-QUIZ!

When the Washington Monument opened in 1888, why were women forced to walk up its 897 steps— many women collapsed, some even died—while men took the steam-driven elevator?

a. A bunch of guys got together and started the rumor that "that's the way George would have wanted it."

b. The elevator was considered too dangerous for women.

c. The right to ride elevators was tied to the right to vote (which women didn't get until years later).

Answer: b (But they were permitted to take pebbles out of their shoes.)

On a first date, wear a T-shirt that says "I'm With Stupid"

OR

a T-shirt that asks "Who Cut the Cheese?"

As punishment during the 1200s, English criminals were often forced to wear a shirt made of hair—it itched like crazy and they rarely ever got a second date.

WHAT DO MOST PEOPLE DO ON A DATE?

"Dates are for having fun, and people should use them to get to know each other. Even boys have something to say if you listen long enough."
Lynette, age 8

Have a fly fisher catch you solidly in the eyeball with his or her hook

OR

have someone jam an ice pick up your nose?

IN 1940, LEON TROTSKY, THE RUSSIAN REVOLUTIONARY, WAS ASSASSINATED IN MEXICO WITH AN ICE PICK. HE SHOULD HAVE GONE FLY-FISHING INSTEAD.

How about golf tees?

"THE FIRST TIME I MET [SYLVESTER STALLONE], HE HAD GOLF TEES UP HIS NOSE. SO I FIGURED WE WERE GOING TO BE OK."

—Sandra Bullock

Forget everyone else's name all the time

OR

have everyone forget your name all the time?

While . . .

Samuel R. Pierce was serving in President Ronald Reagan's cabinet as secretary of the Department of Housing and Urban Development, Reagan failed to recognize him at a White House reception. The president shook Pierce's hand, looked him in the eye, and said, "Hello, Mr. Mayor."

While . . .

singing "The Star-Spangled Banner" at the Liston-Ali match in 1964, Robert Goulet forgot the words. But he did remember his own secretary's name.

If attacked in your home by a burglar, defend yourself with only a baseball bat

OR

an unloaded gun?

Phone (800) 669-9999 and you can add your name to the barrel of an authentic white ash Louisville Slugger. Then, if you come face to face with a burglar, you can watch your own name smash his head. Cool!

In Modesto, California, Steven Richard King was arrested for trying to hold up a bank. He used his thumb and a finger for a gun, but he didn't keep them in his pocket. Hey, if somebody's got to break into your home, Steven's the guy you want. Even with your unloaded gun you're going to look like the smart one.

LASKY: That's not a real gun, is it, Clark?

CLARK GRISWALD: What, are you kidding? This is a Magnum PI.

—FROM *NATIONAL LAMPOON'S VACATION*

Have a Slurpee headache for 12 hours straight

OR

diarrhea for 12 hours straight?

OFFICIAL LIST OF STUFF THAT CAUSES DIARRHEA

CHOLERA (Vibrio cholerae O1)

SHIGELLA (Shigellosis)

ESCHERICHIA COLI (Enterotoxigenic E. coli)

E. COLI O157: H7 (Enterohemorrhagic E. coli)

ESCHERICHIA COLI (Enteroinvasive E. coli)

CLOSTRIDIUM DIFFICILE

BACILLUS CEREUS

SALMONELLA (Salmonellosis)

CAMPYLOBACTER

YERSINIA

GIARDIA LAMBLIA

CRYPTOSPORIDIUM

ENTAMOEBA HISTOLYTICA

ROTAVIRUS

NORWALK AGENT

CALCIVIRUSES

Note: The official list does not include Slurpees.

Have your spouse be disappointed in you

OR

have your child be disappointed in you?

On spousal disappointment . . .

"THE TROUBLE WITH SOME WOMEN IS THAT THEY GET ALL EXCITED ABOUT NOTHING—AND THEN MARRY HIM."

—Cher

"MY DIVORCE CAME AS A COMPLETE SURPRISE TO ME. THAT WILL HAPPEN WHEN YOU HAVEN'T BEEN HOME IN EIGHTEEN YEARS."

—Lee Trevino

On parent-child disappointment . . .

"WHEN I WAS KIDNAPPED, MY PARENTS SNAPPED INTO ACTION. THEY RENTED OUT MY ROOM."

—Woody Allen

"I TAKE MY CHILDREN EVERYWHERE, BUT THEY ALWAYS FIND THEIR WAY BACK HOME."

—Robert Orben

Have a little man
that lives in your mouth and
incessantly hammers
on your teeth with a pick

OR

coexist with a small bird
that lives on your nose
and yanks out your nose hairs
at its discretion?

An old man was sitting on a bench at the park.

A young man walked up and sat down next to him. The young man had a multicolored Mohawk hairdo: green, red, orange, blue, and yellow. The old man stared at him fixedly. The young man turned to him and said, "What's the matter, Old Timer, never done anything wild in your life?"

Without batting an eye, the old man replied, "I got drunk once and had sex with a parrot. I was just wondering if you were my son."

Be seasick for three days straight

OR

be drunk and spinning for four hours straight?

"I WAS SO DRUNK LAST NIGHT, I FELL DOWN AND MISSED THE FLOOR."
—Dean Martin

A guy is going on an ocean cruise, and he tells his doctor that he's worried about getting seasick.

The doctor says, "Just eat two pounds of stewed tomatoes before you leave the dock."

The guy says, "Will that keep me from getting sick, Doc?"

The doctor says, "No, but it'll look real pretty in the water."

Always almost have to sneeze

OR

hit your funny bone every 15 minutes?

Want to be in the *Guinness Book of Records*? Then go with the continuous sneezing:

Donna Griffiths sneezed for 977 days (two-and-a-half million sneezes) between January 13, 1981, and September 16, 1983. And that got her in the book.

Be on vacation with your 60-year-old parents and have your mom insist on wearing a thong bikini

OR

have your dad insist on wearing a tiny, Euro-style bikini bathing suit?

"I'm letting it all hang out— and there's a lot there to hang."

—RODNEY DANGERFIELD, ON WEARING A THONG IN THE FILM *MY 5 WIVES*

"THERE IS NO SUCH THING AS 'FUN FOR THE WHOLE FAMILY.'"

—Jerry Seinfeld

Run (no walking) a half marathon in wooden shoes

OR

bike two hundred miles with no seat, just the post sticking up?

A MARATHON JOKE

Mary was having an affair while her husband worked overtime. One Sunday she was in bed with her boyfriend, Ralph, when she heard her husband's car pull into the driveway. She yelled at Ralph, "Oh my God, my husband's home! Grab your clothes and jump out the window! Hurry!"

Ralph looked out the window and said, "I can't jump out the window! It's pouring rain out there!"

Mary cried, "If my husband catches us in here, he'll kill us!"

So Ralph, still naked, grabbed his clothes and jumped out the window. When he landed outside he found himself in the middle of a marathon race, so he started running alongside the others.

One of the runners asked him, "Do you always run in the nude?"

"Oh yes, it feels so free having the air blow over your skin while you are running," Ralph gasped.

Then another runner asked, "Do you always run carrying your clothes on your arm?"

"Oh yes, that way I can get dressed at the end of the run and get in my car to go home," said Ralph.

Then another runner asked, "Do you always wear a condom when you run?"

"Only if it's raining," replied Ralph.

Bite the curb and get kicked in the back of the head

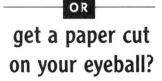

get a paper cut on your eyeball?

MOVIE RENTAL OPPORTUNITY . . .

Rent *American History X* to visualize biting the curb and getting kicked (stomped, actually) in the back of the head.

Synopsis: Edward Norton becomes the leader of a white supremacist group after his father is violently murdered by a black gang member. After spending time in prison (for kicking a guy in the back of the head while the guy bites the curb), Norton no longer wants to be a part of the hate and violence that his neo-Nazi group cultivates, and tries to separate himself and brother Edward Furlong from the urban racism.

> *VITREOUS HUMOR* **IS THE SQUISHY JELLY INSIDE YOUR EYEBALL. IT IS PROTECTED BY THE *SCLERA*, A THICK OUTER SKIN.**

In your teenager's room, find a vial of cocaine

OR

a gun?

Average number of U.S. public-school students expelled for firearm possession each day of the 1997–1998 school year: 22

BY HIS OWN ACCOUNT, TIM RAINES PREFERRED THE HEAD-FIRST SLIDE DURING HIS EARLY YEARS AS A MONTREAL EXPOS BASE STEALER BECAUSE HE HAD VIALS OF COCAINE IN HIS BACK POCKET.

WOULD YOU RATHER...

Be forced to watch
The Sound of Music
continuously for 48 hours

OR

drive cross-country with
Barry Manilow singing
on the radio the whole time?

**REALLY, REALLY SMALL COUNTRIES YOU
CAN HOPE TO BE DRIVING ACROSS**
*(and by the way, good luck,
because some of them are just collections of islands):*

Luxembourg: 998 square miles in area
Fiji: 7,054 square miles in area
Vatican City: 0.2 square miles in area
Micronesia: 271 square miles in area
Liechtenstein: 62 square miles in area

Be stranded on an island for two years with twenty friends of your choice

with a group of twenty famous people of your choosing?

As a young man, the British poet laureate Alfred Lord Tennyson suffered from a terrible bout of hemorrhoids. He visited a young proctologist and was successfully cured.

Years later, after Tennyson had become a successful and well-known poet, he suffered another attack. He returned to the proctologist, expecting to be recognized as the former patient who had become the famous poet. The proctologist, however, showed no sign of recognizing him.

It was only when the great lord bent over to be examined that the proctologist exclaimed, "Ah, Tennyson!"

"IT'S NOT WHERE YOU GO OR WHAT YOU DO, IT'S WHO YOU TAKE ALONG WITH YOU."

—Anonymous

As a man, have your testicles eaten off by a squirrel

your eyeballs pecked out by a bird?

Hitler had only one testicle.
(Too bad the squirrel stopped
so far short of the neck.)

AN OSTRICH'S EYE IS
BIGGER THAN ITS BRAIN.

Have brown teeth

OR

a hairline just one-half inch above your eyebrows?

Popular New York City sportscaster Warner Wolf's false teeth once popped out during a live broadcast. At that moment, Warner would have been very happy with a hairline just one-half inch above his eyebrows.

You have about 100,000 hairs on your head if you're a brunette. It's 150,000 if you're a blond, and 60,000 if you're a redhead.

Live in a world without grass

OR

roads?

"Roads?
Where we're
going we don't
need roads."
—DR. EMMET BROWN,
IN *BACK TO THE FUTURE*

"IF YOU CAN'T
SMOKE IT, YOU
SHOULDN'T
PLAY ON IT."
—Bill Lee, pitcher,
on grass versus
artificial turf

Shove your whole head into an elephant's butt

OR

lick a corpse clean after an autopsy?

Fifth runner-up in the 1999 Darwin Natural Selection Awards went to a San Anselmo, California, man who died when he hit a lift tower at the Mammoth Mountain ski area while riding down the slope on a foam pad. David Hubal, 22, was pronounced dead at Central Mammoth Hospital. The accident occurred about 3 A.M., the Mono County Sheriff's Department said. Hubal and his friends apparently had hiked up a ski run called Stump Alley and untied several yellow foam protectors from lift towers, said Lt. Mike Donnelly of the Mammoth Lakes Police Department. The pads are used to protect skiers who might hit towers. The group apparently used the pads to slide down the ski slope and Hubal crashed into a tower. It has since been determined the tower he hit was the one with its pad removed.

THIS GUY SEEMS TO HAVE HAD HIS HEAD UP HIS OWN YOU-NOW-WHAT . . .

Have a butt full of worms

OR

a mouthful of ticks?

The roundworm *Ascaris* can live inside the human intestines and grow to 16 inches long. The female can lay as many as 200,000 eggs inside a human every day.

A HAIKU BY URKOV

Could someone please run?
Get me a dictionary
Define the word "full"

—Michael Urkov, Redding, CA

Super glue your eyes shut

OR

super glue them open?

"WE COULD NEVER LEARN TO BE BRAVE AND PATIENT, IF THERE WERE ONLY JOY IN THE WORLD."

—Helen Keller

INSTEAD OF STITCHES OR STAPLES, SOME PHYSICIANS NOW USE AN ADHESIVE SIMILAR TO SUPER GLUE BECAUSE "GLUING" LESSENS SCARRING AND DECREASES THE POSSIBILITY OF BACTERIAL INFECTION.

Have a perfect body (excluding your face) above the waist

below the waist?

IN 1989, AN IOWA LICENSING BOARD REFUSED TO REOPEN THE CASE OF AN OPTOMETRIST WHO WAS PLACED ON PROBATION FOR HAVING WOMEN STRIP TO THE WAIST FOR THEIR EYE EXAMINATIONS.

If the Barbie doll was life-size, her measurements would be 39-23-33. She would stand 7 feet 2 inches tall and have a neck twice the length of a normal human's neck. WNBA anyone?

Tell someone famous that his (or her) fly is open

OR

have someone famous tell you your fly is open?

During the fall of 1998, museum-goers unzipped the fly on the Bill Clinton wax figure at Madame Tussaud's in Sydney, Australia, 120 times. At that point, the museum sewed up his trousers.

Hmm. Maybe Hillary should've thought of that.

Be perceived as intelligent

OR

street smart? (but not both)

"A highbrow is a person educated
beyond his intelligence."
—BRANDER MATTHEWS

"Smart is better than lucky."
—TITANIC THOMPSON, *HUSTLER*

"An intellectual is a man who takes more words
than necessary to tell more than he knows."
—DWIGHT EISENHOWER

Need medical attention
because you accidentally got
a large marble stuck in your nose

OR

because you got your head
stuck between the bars of
a wrought iron fence?

A marble up the nose or a head between the bars is nothing. Get a load of this (it's true!):

A man walked into an Ohio police station with a nine-inch wire sticking out of his forehead. Turns out that he had drilled a six-inch-deep hole in his skull with a Black & Decker power drill and stuck the wire in there to see if he could find his missing brain. Having not found it, he headed right to the police station to report his brain as stolen.

**BY THE END OF THIS DAY, 107 INCORRECT
MEDICAL PROCEDURES WILL HAVE BEEN
PERFORMED IN THE UNITED STATES.**

Age only from the neck up

OR

age only from the neck down?

"I HAVE EVERYTHING NOW I HAD 20 YEARS AGO—EXCEPT NOW IT'S ALL LOWER."
—Gypsy Rose Lee

"I PREFER OLD AGE TO THE ALTERNATIVE."
—Maurice Chevalier

Call an important client by the wrong name

OR

blank on your fiance's parents' names when you introduce them to your parents?

The odds of screwing up like this can really vary with the setting.

Setting: China. Go with "Li" and you'll get the name correct at least 87 million times. That's right, Li is the family name for over 87 million people in China.

Setting: Bulgarian national soccer tournament. Mumble anything, but be sure to end with "ov." Bulgaria was the only soccer team in the 1994 World Cup in which all players' last names ended with the letters O-V.

Setting: Calvin and Hobbes comic strip. Suzie Derkins is the only character that has a first and last name. Calvin's parents have no names at all.

Setting: The White House. President Ronald Reagan was always doing stuff like this and people loved him. So co-star with a monkey, run for office, and don't fret!

Constantly be mistaken for the opposite sex

OR

find out that you were voted "Ugliest Classmate" by your entire school?

WHEN JON CLARK, ADOPTED SON OF JAZZ MUSICIAN MR. BILLY TIMPTON, WAS TOLD BY THE UNDERTAKER THAT HIS FATHER WAS A WOMAN, CLARK SAID, "TO ME, HE'LL ALWAYS BE DAD."

"I WAS SO UGLY WHEN I WAS BORN THAT THE DOCTOR SLAPPED MY MOTHER."

—Henny Youngman

Turn around three times before you sit down anywhere

OR

do a little jig before you go through any doorway?

"A boy can learn a lot from a dog: obedience, loyalty, and the importance of turning around three times before lying down."

—ROBERT BENCHLEY

Drink and dance and laugh and lie,
Love, the reeling midnight through.
For tomorrow we shall die!
(But, alas, we never do.)

—DOROTHY PARKER, "THE FLAW IN
PAGANISM," IN *DEATH AND TAXES*

As a man, crap a softball

OR

pee a marble?

The huge college freshman figured he'd try out for the football team.

"Can you tackle?" asked the coach.

"Watch this," said the freshman, who proceeded to run smack into a telephone pole, shattering it to splinters.

"Wow," said the coach. "I'm impressed. Can you run?"

"Of course I can run," said the freshman. He was off like a shot, and in just over nine seconds, he had run a hundred-yard dash.

"Great!" enthused the coach. "But can you pass a football?"

The freshman rolled his eyes, hesitated for a few seconds. "Well, sir," he said, "if I can swallow it, I can probably pass it."

THE SLANG WORD *CRAP* COMES FROM THOMAS CRAPPER, THE MAN CREDITED WITH INVENTING THE MODERN TOILET.

Eat five extremely green bananas (green enough that the peel breaks off instead of bending)

OR

eat five extremely overripe bananas (with an entirely brown peel and the actual fruit all brown and mushy)?

AMERICANS EAT 12 BILLION BANANAS A YEAR.

BRAD PITT AND JENNIFER ANISTON WROTE THEIR OWN WEDDING VOWS, WHICH INCLUDED HER PROMISE TO ALWAYS MAKE HIS "FAVORITE BANANA MILKSHAKE."

If your bananas are too green, you can put them in a brown paper bag to ripen. They will produce ethylene gas, which hastens the ripening process. If you add an apple or tomato to the bag, the bananas will ripen even faster. (Turbo banana ripening!)

Mosquitoes are more likely to bite you right after you've eaten a banana.

Have a hidden video camera
at work (with audio!)
catch you hacking up a big,
ugly ball of phlegm
and then looking at it

OR

passing gas and then making
a face reacting to the smell?

President Ronald Reagan's
attorney general, Ed Meese,
advised all employers to spy
on workers in "locker rooms,
parking lots, shipping and
mail room areas and even
the nearby taverns" to catch
them using drugs.

IN 1980,
A PROFESSIONAL
JAPANESE FARTER
CAPTIVATED AUDIENCES
DURING A TELEVISED
PERFORMANCE BY FARTING
3,000 TIMES IN A ROW,
IMITATING SOUNDS,
AND PLAYING SONGS.

Chew a piece of toenail off a dirty man's foot

OR

thoroughly lick his unshowered armpit?

When people are between 20 and 40 years old or pregnant, their toenails grow faster than everybody else's. And when people are ill, their toenails grow slower.

AS FOR LICKING SWEATY ARMPITS, UNDERARM PERSPIRATION CONTAINS MORE THAN 100 CHEMICALS. SO THINK OF IT THIS WAY: IT'S LIKE LICKING POPULAR BREAKFAST CEREALS.

Be incredibly attractive physically
but exude an extremely
bothersome odor

OR

be hideously unattractive
but have a scent that is
irresistible?

BROMOHYPERHIDROSIS
IS A CONDITION
THAT CAUSES EXCESSIVE,
FOUL-SMELLING SWEATING.

WHEN NAPOLEON BONAPARTE
HEADED HOME TO TAKE A
BREAK FROM CONQUERING THE
WORLD, HE WROTE AHEAD TO
HIS WIFE, JOSEPHINE, ASKING
HER NOT TO BATHE. HE LIKED
HER STINKY ODOR.

Cut ¼ acre of grass with your teeth

lick up a 15-foot-by-15-foot rain puddle?

In order to digest grass, cows chew, swallow, and vomit it (then repeat, up to four times) as it proceeds through the four chambers of their stomachs.

A HAIKU BY URKOV

A suburban lawn?
Pristine liquid from heaven?
Dogs should wear diapers.

—Michael Urkov, Redding, CA

Eat a cup of uncooked popcorn

OR

a box of uncooked spaghetti?

RULES OF THUMB

To get oil hot enough to pop corn, place three kernels in the oil as it heats; when all three pop, the oil is hot enough. You should get 34 cups of popped corn from a pound of kernels. Top-quality kernels will give you an extra 10 cups.

Your thumb and index finger will encircle four modest servings of uncooked spaghetti. When spaghetti is done, it will stick to the wall.

As a woman, have real, although low hanging, 34-Ds

OR

have uppity, obnoxiously fake 34-Ds?

GREAT MOVIE LINES GREATLY
IMPROVED BY SUBSTITUTING "34-Ds"

"Oh, no, it wasn't the airplanes—
it was 34-Ds that killed the beast."
—*KING KONG*

"LOOKING AT
CLEAVAGE IS
LIKE LOOKING
AT THE SUN.
YOU DON'T
STARE AT IT.
YOU GET A
SENSE AND
THEN LOOK
AWAY."

—Jerry Seinfeld

"I coulda been a 34-D."
—*ON THE WATERFRONT*

"You're not too smart—are you?
I like that in a 34-D."
—*BODY HEAT*

Streak naked through your office

be known as the office farter?

Bernard Clemmens of London managed to sustain a fart for an officially recorded time of 2 minutes and 42 seconds.

THE AVERAGE PERSON FARTS ABOUT 14 TIMES A DAY.

BECAUSE FARTING IN A SPACE SUIT WILL DAMAGE IT, ASTRONAUTS ARE NOT ALLOWED TO EAT BEANS BEFORE THEY GO INTO SPACE.

Have frequent spurts of uncontrollable drooling

OR

be a bed wetter?

Chewing on cinnamon bark for a day is a popular folk remedy for curing bed-wetting.

Give someone the finger
when he cuts you off in his car
and have him turn out to be
your priest or rabbi

OR

have your friends catch you
picking up trash while you're
wearing a felon-orange jumpsuit?

The problem with randomly "giving the finger" is that it's been around for a long time—even the Romans were using it at the time of Christ. So everybody knows what it means, even religious guys like priests and rabbis.

"YOU KNOW WHAT A FRIEND IS? SOMEONE WHO KNOWS ALL ABOUT YOU AND LIKES YOU ANYWAY."
—Duane Charles Parcells

REBECCA: "Guess what I kept seeing as I was driving in to work just now?"

CARLA: "The middle finger of every driver in Boston?"
—FROM CHEERS

Have heinous breath and good teeth

gross teeth and regular breath?

Clark Gable had false teeth, heinous breath, and lots of good-looking women in his life.

Austin Powers has gross teeth, regular breath (presumably), and lots of good-looking women in his life.

Therefore, Jim Purol—who in 1983 simultaneously smoked 140 cigarettes for five minutes—must have been a real babe magnet.

Talk like
you have walnuts
in your mouth

OR

walk like
you have a walnut
up your butt?

Jose Luis Astoreka of Spain holds
the world record for cracking walnuts
between the cheeks of his butt
(30 in 57 seconds).

As a woman and in front of
a crowd of friends, have to crush
ten empty beer cans
against your forehead

OR

mud wrestle a friend
while you are both in bikinis?

IN THE YEAR 2000,
STORES STARTED SELLING
BEER IN PLASTIC BOTTLES.

"AN INJURED
FRIEND IS
THE BITTEREST
OF FOES."

—Thomas Jefferson

For the post-event party, why not rent . . .
Wrestling Women vs. the Aztec Mummy (1959):
Women, broad of shoulder, wrestle an ancient
Aztec wrestler who comes to life. Rereleased with
a new rock soundtrack as *Rock 'n' Roll Wrestling
Women vs. the Aztec Mummy.* (Like that helped.)

Have a bird that says
"f_ _ _ you"
every time someone walks
into the room

have a dog that
humps all of your guests' legs?

FRENCH PAINTER PAUL CEZANNE
(1839–1906) GOT A PARROT AND
TAUGHT IT TO REPEATEDLY SAY
"CEZANNE IS A GREAT PAINTER!"

Q: WHY WERE MEN GIVEN LARGER
BRAINS THAN DOGS?

A: SO THEY WOULDN'T HUMP WOMEN'S
LEGS AT COCKTAIL PARTIES.

Have a lisp

OR

pronounce your Rs as Ws?

PUNK POETRY RESEARCH

Normal: "Out of my way or I'll wreck your day."
With lisp: "Out of my way or I'll wreck your day." (Not bad.)
Rs as Ws: "Out of my way ow I'll weck youw day." (Not bad.)

Normal: "I'd feel so much better with my hand up your sweater."
With lisp: "I'd feel tho much better with my hand up your thweater." (Hmmm.)
Rs as Ws: "I'd feel so much bettew with my hand up youw sweatew." (Not bad.)

The *Washington Post* recently had a contest for readers in which they were asked to supply alternative meanings for various words. The following was one of the winning entries:
Lymph (v.): to walk with a lisp

As a woman, have a really hairy back

OR

really long, curly, exposed nose hairs?

THERE ARE OVER 5,000,000 HAIRS ON YOUR BODY.

A HAIKU BY URKOV

Is hair not power?
Excess testosterone, gift?
Embrace its lush fields.

—Michael Urkov, Redding, CA

A DANGLING CURL OF HAIR IS KNOWN AS A "FEAT."

Get caught by your spouse, in bed with your lover

OR

get caught by the press, embezzling money from the charity over which you preside?

Press attention lasts until
a better story comes along.

But an ex-wife is forever.

In 1996, 22% of
Americans said
that adultery can
sometimes be good
for the marriage.

Every day for a year, have to wear either the same pair of unwashed underwear

OR

the same pair of unwashed socks?

IN 1984, THE JAPANESE INVENTED UNDERWEAR TO BE WORN FOR SIX DAYS STRAIGHT: "THE WEARER ROTATES IT 120 DEGREES EACH DAY, AND THEN WEARS IT INSIDE OUT FOR ANOTHER THREE."

THE AVERAGE PERSON LOSES ABOUT ONE SOCK PER LOAD OF LAUNDRY.

Be known for being cheap

OR

for being a crybaby?

At a graveyard near Cincinnati, three mourners—a contractor, a doctor, and a lawyer—joined the grieving widow at the service for their close friend. The widow asked if each would place an offering in her husband's casket, as this had long been a family tradition.

The contractor nodded and then said a short prayer before placing a hundred-dollar bill in the casket.

The doctor, nearly in tears, also placed a hundred-dollar bill in the casket.

Then the lawyer scribbled out a check for three hundred dollars, put it in the casket, and pocketed the two hundred dollars in cash.

According to a new study, men cry an average of once a month.

Gee, we wonder what time of the month that would be. . . .

Have a small butt on your forehead

OR

two little feet dangling beneath your chin?

Some butterflies have fake heads on their butts to confuse hungry predators.

In some cultures, feet are sexy. An archaic law in rural China prohibits any male from looking at the bare feet of another man's wife. Men are allowed to see anything else they want, even the woman's naked body. But, according to the tradition, if a neighbor or relative steals a glance at a woman's toes, her husband is obligated to kill him.

Always pick your nose immediately before shaking hands

OR

constantly have one hand, including your wrist, down your pants?

GREETING SOMEBODY WITH AN OPEN HAND COMES FROM THE DAYS WHEN YOU HAD TO BE SURE THAT THE OTHER GUY WASN'T HOLDING A WEAPON.

IN INDONESIA, THE PENALTY FOR MASTURBATION IS DECAPITATION.

Have to watch, with your friends, a video of every argument you've ever had with your siblings

every argument you've ever had with your parents?

"CHILDREN TODAY ARE TYRANTS.
THEY CONTRADICT THEIR PARENTS,
GOBBLE THEIR FOOD AND
TYRANNIZE THEIR TEACHERS."

—Socrates (470–399 B.C.)

NEVER ARGUE
WITH IDIOTS.
THEY DRAG YOU
DOWN TO THEIR
LEVEL, THEN
BEAT YOU WITH
EXPERIENCE.

Have to watch, with your family
and friends, a video of every
time you have ever cursed

OR

every time you have ever lied?

A round-up of the language used by Eddie Murphy
in his one-hour TV comedy special RAW:

SWEAR WORD	NUMBER OF TIMES USED
1. S@#!	103
2. F%/&	92
3. Motherf%/&er	56
4. A##	50
5. F%/&ing	39
6. D#&k	33
7. F%/&ed up/f%/&ed	28
8. Pu##y	28
9. Motherf%/&ing	22
10. Bitch	18
11. Goddamn/damn	17
12. Bulls@#!	4
TOTAL	490

Have no short-term memory

OR

no long-term memory?

"CLINTON LIED. A MAN MIGHT FORGET WHERE HE PARKS OR WHERE HE LIVES, BUT HE NEVER FORGETS ORAL SEX, NO MATTER HOW BAD IT IS."

—Barbara Bush

For many years
have terrible acne
that will go away when you're 30

OR

for life have a birthmark
the size of a quarter
in the middle of your forehead?

A HAIKU BY URKOV

Look close, grow cross-eyed
Evil volcano throbbing
Ready to erupt

—Michael Urkov, Redding, CA

You can get a quarter through a hole the size of a nickel.
Seriously. Trace a nickel on a sheet of paper and cut out
the circle. Fold the paper in half so that the nickel-size hole
is on the fold. Place the quarter inside the fold, in the
nickel's hole, so it looks like its butt is hanging out. Pull
the corners of the paper up. The hole will widen and the
quarter will fall through. Cool!

Spend the night enclosed in a coffin in your bedroom

OR

be locked inside a funeral home for the night but free to wander?

A DEATH JOKE

A grieving widow goes into a funeral home to make arrangements for her husband's funeral. She tells the director that her husband must be buried in a blue suit. The director asks, "Wouldn't it just be easier to bury him in the black suit that he's wearing?" The widow insists it be a blue suit and gives the director a blank check to buy one.

When she returns for the wake, she sees her husband in the coffin and he is wearing a beautiful blue suit. She thanks the director and asks him how much it cost. He says, "Actually, it didn't cost anything. The funniest thing happened. As soon as you left, another corpse was brought in, this one wearing a blue suit. I noticed that they were about the same size, and asked the other widow if she would mind if her husband was buried in a black suit. She said that was fine with her. So . . . I switched the heads."

Have one long, thick, furry eyebrow across your entire forehead

OR

an inordinate amount of ear and nose hair that cannot be removed?

In the 1700s, many women considered it fashionable to wear fake eyebrows made of mouse fur.

WHAT DO POP SINGER MICHAEL JACKSON AND THE *MONA LISA* HAVE IN COMMON? NO EYEBROWS.

As a man,
accidentally lose control
of your bowels
during a prostate examination

OR

get an erection
during a hernia check?

In 1984, the New York
Board of Regents
disciplined a physician
for performing bladder
and prostate operations
after becoming blind.
The great thing was that
he couldn't see if you
had an erection or not.

A skunk's stench
is created when
it releases an oily
yellow liquid from
one of two small
sacs on either side
of its anus. It can
shoot the liquid
to distances of
up to 12 feet.

Have to walk to the end of your driveway nude every day to get your mail

OR

have your spouse walk to the mailbox in the nude?

LIBERALS GO SKINNY-DIPPING AT THE RATE OF 28 PER 100, WHEREAS ONLY 15% OF CONSERVATIVES SAY THEY'VE GONE SKINNY-DIPPING.*

WHO SLEEPS
IN THE NUDE:
26% OF MEN
AND
6% OF WOMEN

A patent's been awarded for the invention of boots with pockets. It was designed and developed for nudists. (You could use that pocket to take the mailman's holiday tip down to the end of the driveway.)

*Liberals, therefore, are more likely to swim naked to their mailboxes.

Be freed by the fire department
after your hand got caught
in the toilet bowl
(while dressed)

 OR

after your finger got caught
in the shower head
(while naked)?

Be the naked Minnesota couple whom
firefighters had to rescue after a sofa folded
shut around them while they duplicated
a "stupid human trick"
from the *David Letterman Show*.

 -OR-

Be 326-pound President William Howard Taft,
who got stuck in the White House bathtub.

Walk barefoot over six feet of holly leaves

over six feet of live roaches?

THERE'S A COCKROACH HALL OF FAME IN PLANO, TEXAS. FOR DIRECTIONS AND HOURS, PHONE (912) 519-0355. SADLY, THERE IS NOT A HOLLY HALL OF FAME. (HOLLY OF FAME?)

A COCKROACH CAN LIVE FOR 9 DAYS WITHOUT ITS HEAD BEFORE IT STARVES TO DEATH.

As a woman, be totally flat chested with saucer-size nipples

OR

have huge breasts with no nipples?

Desktop Reference Opportunity!

In 1985, Westwood Publishing Company published the book *Natural Breast Enlargement with Total Mind Power: How to Use the Other 90 Percent of Your Mind to Increase the Size of Your Breasts.*

IT IS REPORTED BY *THE WORLD OF MEDICINE* THAT ONE 30-YEAR-OLD WOMAN HAD NATURAL BREASTS THAT WEIGHED IN AT FIFTY-TWO POUNDS.

As a man, have hair implants that are totally obvious

OR

a toupee that is a bad match to your remaining hair?

"THERE'S NO SENSE IN PUTTING A ROOF ON AN EMPTY SHED."

—proverb

Histiaeos, a governor in ancient Greece, sent secret messages by shaving a slave's head, tattooing a message on it, waiting for the hair to grow back, then sending the slave off to deliver the message. Secretive? Yes. Express delivery? No.

The personnel directors of America's hundred largest companies were asked to describe their most unusual experience interviewing prospective employees. One executive reported:

"A balding candidate excused himself and returned to the office a few minutes later wearing a hairpiece."

Do a mini cheer whenever someone compliments you

OR

have to jump up and touch the door frame every time you go through a door?

"I'M THE KING OF THE WORLD!"

—James Cameron, director, upon receiving an Oscar for *Titanic*

And speaking of jumping, from September 30 to October 4, 1985, Mark Harrison and Tony Lunn played over 101 hours of hopscotch.

Wake up nude and unharmed
on a park bench and
have no idea of how
you got there

OR

expecting a costume party,
dress as a giant banana for
a black tie affair and
have to stay the whole night?

A beautiful blonde walked into the costume party completely
naked. Her alarmed host rushed to stop her at the door as
everyone turned to stare.

"Where's your costume?" he hissed through clenched teeth.

"This is it," she calmly explained. "I came as Adam."

"Adam?" her host exploded.

"You don't even have a dick!"

"I just got here, Nigel,"
she replied. "Give me
a few minutes."

"It's not true
I had nothing
on. I had the
radio on."

—MARILYN MONROE

Never look healthy

 OR

never feel healthy?

When designer Coco Chanel was photographed with tanned skin in the late 1930s, being tan suddenly became a fashionable and healthy look for whites and no longer the undesirable look of a downtrodden field laborer.

Go to your high school reunion a multimillionaire but 200 pounds overweight

OR

poor but in perfect shape?

IS YOUR HIGH SCHOOL REUNION IN THE UKRAINE? BECAUSE NOT SO LONG AGO, THE EXCHANGE RATE WAS RUNNING AT 428,287.55 UKRAINIAN KARBOVANETS TO THE DOLLAR. WHICH MEANS THAT IF YOU HAD TOTAL ASSETS OF JUST $5.62, YOU COULD HAVE BEEN A UKRAINIAN MILLIONAIRE.

Speaking of showing up a bit overweight, the heaviest man in medical history was Jon Brower Minnoch (1941–1983). Weighing as much as 1,387 pounds, Jon didn't go anywhere, let alone to some Ukrainian high school reunion.

Lick the head of a bald Harley biker after a sweaty race

OR

lick the surface of an entire car hood that hasn't been washed in a month?

PILGARLIC IS THE FANCY WORD FOR A BALD HEAD THAT LOOKS LIKE A PEELED GARLIC.

Think about this: Mosquitoes can fly well enough to stay dry in the rain, yet they can't avoid your oncoming windshield on the highway. How lame is that?

FASTEST SPEED THE AVERAGE GUY HAS DRIVEN:
116.7 MPH

Stutter badly

OR

drool noticeably?

Sportscaster Frank Gifford was known for stuttering and stumbling at least once during every broadcast. For instance, he said Atlanta Falcons coach Leeman Bennet's name as "Leeman Beeman" almost every time he said it. Gifford even began one broadcast by saying, "Hi, Frank, I'm everybody."

Get everywhere by crawling

OR

have to stand on your hands when you are stationary?

Crawling
is considered to be
"progression with one or
the other knee in unbroken
contact with the ground."

Longest *continuous* crawl is 28.5 miles.

Farthest crawl—870 miles—was done over 15 months from Aligarh to Jammu, India, by some Indian guy.

Be incapable of love

honesty?

"LOVE IS A GRAVE MENTAL DISEASE."
—Plato

"PLATO IS A BORE."
—Nietzsche

If you had to come up with $50,000 in five days to get a sibling out of jail, try to steal it

OR

go to Vegas?

WHILE INCARCERATED IN 1993, MIKE TYSON USED THE PRISON PAY PHONE TO NEGOTIATE HIS PURCHASE OF A LAMBORGHINI DIABLO.

In 1982, the video game Pac Man was so popular that it was named Time *magazine's "man" of the year. That year, Americans spent more than $6 billion in quarters on the arcade game—more than they spent in Las Vegas casinos and movie theaters combined.*

Have your parents walk in on you having sex

walk in on your parents having sex?

**PARENTS HAVE SEX?
SINCE WHEN?**

Sweat green liquid from your pores

OR

fart blue smoke?

THE FIRST ADVERTISEMENT
EVER TO MENTION BODY ODOR
WAS FOR THE DEODORANT ODORONO.

One of France's leading stage performers
of the late 1800s was Joseph Pujol,
known as "Le Pétomane" (the Fartiste).
His farting act included songs, various
imitations, and the sounds of battle.

Go to junior high one day wearing only your tight white underwear

OR

after being sprayed by a skunk?

In 1934, Clark Gable removed his shirt in *It Happened One Night* and revealed that he wasn't wearing an undershirt. Undershirt sales took a dive.

In 1951, Marlon Brando looked great in his form-fitting undershirt in *A Streetcar Named Desire*. Undershirt sales took off.

In 1994, Pee-Wee Herman wore a skunk and . . . never mind.

Get stood up for your high school prom

OR

take the date you dreamt of to the prom and have him or her leave with someone else?

Dreamt is the only English word that ends in the letters M-T. (It's sharing tidbits of trivia like this that'll cause your prom date to leave with someone else.)

"I have such poor vision that I can date anybody."
—GARRY SHANDLING

While drunk, go rock climbing

OR

learn how to surf?

"IF YOU DRINK, DON'T DRIVE. DON'T EVEN PUTT."
—Dean Martin

MUNICH, GERMANY—A man was convicted for operating his electric wheelchair while drunk (three times the legal blood-alcohol limit). His sentence: a three-month ban on driving his wheelchair and any other vehicle and a two-month suspended jail sentence.

Wet the bed
when you're with your partner for the first time

OR

wet your pants in a college class?

BUZZ ALDRIN WAS THE FIRST MAN TO PEE IN HIS PANTS ON THE MOON. HOWEVER, HE WAS NOT IN BED WITH NEIL ARMSTRONG AT THE TIME.

AS FOR PEEING IN YOUR PANTS IN COLLEGE, IT'S NO BIG DEAL. AFTER ALL, 27% OF AMERICAN MALE COLLEGE STUDENTS BELIEVE LIFE IS A MEANINGLESS EXISTENTIAL HELL. SO WHAT'S A BIT OF PEE?

> A little old man says to his doctor, "You gotta help me. Every morning at seven o'clock I take a nice long pee, and then at eight, just like clockwork, I take a big healthy crap."
> The doctor says, "What's the problem?"
> "I don't get up till nine."

Be a woman with a mustache

OR

a man with large breasts?

The fact is that every woman once had a mustache—about four months before birth, when hair—known as lanugo— grows all over a kid's hairy-as-an-ape body. (It then falls out about a month before birth. Thank God!)

The fact is that men's nipples have the anatomical equipment in place to provide milk. (But the process lies dormant unless stimulated by the female hormone estrogen. Thank God!)

Have five bottles stuck on the fingers of one hand for a year

OR

a bucket stuck on your foot for a year?

It depends . . .

If you're Anne Boleyn (Queen Elizabeth I's mother), with six fingers on one hand, those five bottles leave one finger free. Not bad.

If you had the bottles on your right hand . . . you could still type "stewardesses" because it is the longest word that is typed with only the left hand.

Sit naked on a pedestal in the middle of a crowded public park

OR

sit naked on a platter with an apple in your mouth at a gala dinner party?

ST. SIMEON THE YOUNGER, A MONK,
SAT ON A STONE TOWER
FROM THE YEARS 521 TO 597.

THERE'S
CYANIDE
IN APPLE
SEEDS.

In 1992, Frank Perkins of Los Angeles tried to break the world flagpole-sitting record. A horrible bout with the flu caused him to come down eight hours short of the 400-day record.

As a man, be stinking drunk at the birth of your first child

OR

have the worst hangover of your life on your wedding day?

On the morning he was to baptize a baby, the minister approached the young father and said solemnly, "Baptism is a serious step. Are you prepared for it?"

"I think so," the man replied. "My wife made a ham last night and we have a caterer coming this morning with hors d'oeuvres, pasta salad, and a turkey."

"I don't mean that," the minister responded. "I mean, are you prepared spiritually?"

"Sure," said the young dad. "I've got a keg of beer and three liters of tequila."

HEAVIEST BOOZING YEAR FOR THE AVERAGE MAN: AGE 30.

Get stood up at the altar

OR

have someone stand up during your wedding and reveal that your spouse-to-be has been cheating?

FRED: "So, how was your wedding night?"

TED: "Very good until the morning after. I forgot where I was and I said to my wife, 'You were wonderful. Here's $100.'"

FRED: "That's not that bad. She might not guess that you thought she was a hooker."

TED: "But she gave me back $50 and said, 'Keep the change.'"

Be a 12-year-old still in third grade who's liked by classmates and teachers

OR

a 12-year-old in college who's considered a total freak?

THINK ABOUT IT THIS WAY: WHICH FLICK IS MORE FUN TO WATCH?

Billy Madison
Rich kid Adam Sandler goes back to elementary school. Critics lavished this one with accolades like "lame," "infantile," "silly," and "features bodily functions."

Little Man Tate
A child genius is torn between his working-class mother and the domineering director of a school for exceptional children. "Moving, emphatic, bittersweet."—Leonard Maltin

Date someone who talks too loudly

OR

someone who looks like he or she is constantly staring?

When Verona Berkley and her boyfriend, Willie Bradley, couldn't agree on what to watch on TV, *The Thorn Birds* or a basketball game, she killed him.

> "IT IS BETTER TO KEEP YOUR MOUTH SHUT AND APPEAR STUPID THAN TO OPEN IT AND REMOVE ALL DOUBT."
>
> —Mark Twain

Have a see-through nose

OR

entirely white eyeballs?

If you've got white eyeballs and somebody looks at you, what they'll see is, well, white. But if you've got a see-through nose, what they'll see is:

SEPTUM
(thin wall that divides the nasal cavity)

MUCUS MEMBRANE
(moist tissue that makes a quart of snot every day)

TURBINATES
(small bones that help trap dirt)

20 MILLION OLFACTORY CELLS
(they "smell" the air)

CILIA
(tiny hairs that move back and forth, trapping crud and pushing snot toward the throat)

BOOGERS
(dirt covered by mucus that's begun to dry)

Not eat for three days

OR

not sleep for three days?

YOU'LL DIE FROM TOTAL LACK OF SLEEP SOONER (ABOUT TEN DAYS) THAN FROM STARVATION (A FEW WEEKS). AS FOR JUST THREE DAYS OF EACH, WHAT HAPPENS IS THAT YOU GET REALLY HUNGRY AND REALLY TIRED.

NAPOLEON ONCE DECIDED THAT SLEEP WAS A WASTE OF TIME AND DECLARED THAT FROM THAT MOMENT ON, HE SIMPLY WOULDN'T SLEEP ANYMORE. HE FELL ASLEEP 48 HOURS LATER.

Have to walk on five-foot stilts for the rest of your life

OR

always have to ride a unicycle to get around?

Deepak Lele unicycled the 3,963 miles between New York and Los Angeles in about three-and-a-half months.

JOE BOWEN STILTED THE 3,008 MILES BETWEEN BOWEN, KENTUCKY, AND LOS ANGELES IN ABOUT SIX MONTHS.

Run over your daughter's new puppy

OR

forget her birthday for two consecutive years?

When an elderly London woman's beloved cat became stuck in a tree, a group of British soldiers came to the rescue. The woman was so thankful to have her cat returned safely that she invited the soldiers in for tea. As they drove off afterward, the soldiers backed over the cat and killed it. There's a day that old lady will never forget.

KIDS' ADVICE TO KIDS

"Never trust a dog to watch your food." *Patrick, age 10*

"Puppies still have bad breath even after eating a Tic-Tac." *Joey, age 9*

"Never try to baptize a cat." *Patrick, age 10*

Clip
a homeless stranger's
disgusting toenails

OR

clip
your own toenails
and eat the clippings?

MORE THAN 15%
OF AMERICANS
SECRETLY BITE
THEIR TOENAILS.

Eat a newly born baby rodent

OR

a small sack of crawling caterpillars?

NOTE: AS FOR WHAT FOLLOWS, IT MAY HELP IF YOU'RE OVER 60. BY AGE 60 MOST PEOPLE HAVE LOST HALF OF THEIR TASTE BUDS.

Caterpillar Crunch

1 cup roasted insects (caterpillars, grasshoppers, bees, ants, what have you)	½ cup butter ½ cup honey Large bowl of popped popcorn

1. Mix the insects with the popcorn.
2. Slowly heat butter and honey and mix well; pour over the insect/popcorn mixture and stir well.
3. Spread mixture on a cookie sheet and bake at 350 degrees for 10 minutes.
4. Cut in small pieces and serve.

As a man, find out that your fly was open all day

OR

that your shirt tail was out, you missed a belt loop, and your pants leg was stuck inside the top of your sock?

TEN LINES FROM *STAR WARS* THAT ARE A LOT BETTER IF THE WORD "PANTS" IS TRADED IN

1. "Lock the door and hope they don't have pants."
2. "You are unwise to lower your pants."
3. "I used to bulls-eye womp-rats in my pants back home."
4. "You came in those pants? You're braver than I thought."
5. "Don't worry. Chewie and I have gotten into a lot of pants more heavily guarded than this."
6. "That blast came from those pants. That thing's operational!"
7. "Maybe you'd like it back in my pants, your highness."
8. "These pants may not look like much, kid, but they've got it where it counts."
9. "A tremor in the pants. The last time I felt this was in the presence of my old master."
10. "These pants contain the ultimate power in the Universe. I suggest we use it."

Drink a glass of your own day-old spit

OR

your own sweat?

IF YOU SPIT FROM A STANDING POSITION AND IT FREEZES BEFORE HITTING THE GROUND, IT'S AT LEAST 40 DEGREES BELOW ZERO (FAHRENHEIT).

Human bodies actually contain anywhere from 2 million to 4 million sweat glands, which cover every square inch of the body except the lips.

Be held in high esteem
by one and only one person
whom you truly respect

OR

by 10,000 people that you don't?

OR just the opposite . . .
These individual quotes were reportedly taken
from actual employee performance evaluations in
a large U.S. corporation.

1. "Since my last report, this employee has reached
   rock bottom . . . and has started to dig."

2. "This employee is depriving a village somewhere
   of an idiot."

3. "Got a full 6-pack, but lacks the plastic thing to
   hold it all together."

4. "He doesn't have ulcers, but he's a carrier."

5. "This employee is really not so much of a
   'has-been,' but more of a definite 'won't be.'"

As a brazen, reckless teenager showing off on a class camping trip, drink a thimbleful of snake venom

OR

eat the tail off a dead scorpion?

Snake Scenario

You'll know you've been drinking the venom of a pit viper, cottonmouth, rattlesnake, copperhead, or coral snake (any other snake makes for a pretty boring challenge) should you react with immediate pain and burning in the mouth, swelling, nausea and vomiting, dizziness, weakness, sweats and chills, metallic or rubbery taste in the mouth, paralysis, cardiac arrest or respiratory failure, drowsiness, blurred vision, slurred speech, salivation, and/or seizures.

Scorpion Scenario

Only the *Centruroides sculpturatus's* (a.k.a. the bark scorpion) venom is a neurotoxin (other scorpions cause only local reactions). You'll know you've been eating the tail of a *Centruroides sculpturatus* if you suddenly react with muscle spasms, excessive salivation, fever, blurred vision, slurred speech, wheezing, and seizures.

The good news is that you're a teenager. Children under one year of age almost always die. Children under five often die. Thereafter, you tend to survive with proper medical treatment.

Regardless, there's just got to be some better way of showing off.

For the rest of your life, choose the same drink and the same meal to ingest every time you eat

OR

have someone else always choose what you eat?

At the age of 42, a "Mrs. H." complained of a "slight abdominal pain." Turned out that she had 2,533 objects, including 947 bent pins, in her stomach. They were removed.

A SOUTH AFRICAN MAN ONCE HAD **212** OBJECTS—INCLUDING **53** TOOTHBRUSHES, **2** TELESCOPIC AERIALS, **2** RAZORS, AND **150** HANDLES OF DISPOSABLE RAZORS— REMOVED FROM HIS STOMACH.

Have to slurp
the spittle out of the instruments
of the brass section of
a philharmonic orchestra
after a performance

OR

have to chew the petrified gum
stuck to the bottom of every seat
in a movie theater?

Every year the
average American
chews 190 sticks
of gum.

EVERY HUMAN
PRODUCES
ENOUGH SALIVA
IN HIS OR HER
LIFETIME TO FILL
TWO SWIMMING
POOLS.

Have to put to sleep five puppies you just got

OR

a dog you've had for a year?

"Dogs come when they're called; cats take a message and get back to you."
—MARY BLY

"CATS ARE SMARTER THAN DOGS. YOU CAN'T GET EIGHT CATS TO PULL A SLED THROUGH THE SNOW."
—Jeff Valdez

Drink one gallon of milk, and then ride a roller coaster

OR

ride a roller coaster behind someone who drank one gallon of milk?

SELECT SYNONYMS FOR PUKE:

barf

boot

ralph

technicolor yawn

drive the porcelain bus

yak

upchuck

vomit

toss your cookies

blow chunks

hurl

heave

On the job, be accused of stealing

OR

sexual harassment?

Over 7,500 copies of *Catcher in the Rye* have been checked out of public libraries in Chicago and never returned.

"WHEN A MAN TALKS DIRTY TO A WOMAN, IT'S SEXUAL HARASSMENT; BUT WHEN A WOMAN TALKS DIRTY TO A MAN, IT'S $3.95 PER MINUTE."

—George Carlin

Swallow a small fish
tied to a string and
pull it back up after 3 minutes

OR

gently swallow a live cockroach
whole so that it lives until
it reaches your stomach
(no beverages or chewing allowed)?

**Pnigophobia
is the fear
of choking
on fish bones.**

**THE GASTRIC JUICE
IN YOUR STOMACH IS
PRODUCED BY MORE
THAN 35 MILLION
GLANDS IN YOUR
STOMACH'S LINING.**

WOULD YOU RATHER...

Have a job swabbing
athlete's foot cultures
from between peoples' toes

OR

taking photographs of
skin conditions for
a medical publication?

DISPATCHES FROM THE FOOT FRONT

HAMMERTOE: a deformed toe that buckles up at the middle joint
GANGRENE: massive dead tissue caused by lack of blood
TINEA PEDIS: athlete's foot
PLANTAR WART: foot wart caused by virus
HALLUX VARUS: a condition where the big toe bends away from the others
BUNIONETTE: a bunion of the fifth (pinkie) toe

DISPATCHES FROM THE SKIN FRONT

LEPROSY: a bacterial disease that causes deformities.
KELOIDS: overgrown scars
HIDRADENITIS SUPPURATIVA: inflamed, pus-filled armpits and groin
EHLERS-DANLOS' SYNDROME: symptoms include baggy and easily bruised skin
GENITAL WARTS: (self-explanatory)
DERMATOSIOPHOBIA: fear of skin disease

Eat one long strand of spaghetti that you've sucked through your nose

OR

have a teaspoon of sugar poured into your ear?

Think about this: Mucus (snot!) that coats the skin and hairs inside your nose traps dirt and germs. Cilia—the tiny hairs that line the inside of your nose—push the snot toward the throat and into the stomach, where chemicals destroy most of the trapped bacteria.

CERUMEN IS DOCTORESE FOR EARWAX.

People who live in highly polluted areas produce significantly more earwax than those who live in cleaner environments.

Eat 30 cigarette butts that you find lying on a beach

OR

eat five pounds of wet leaves that you find on the ground after a rainstorm?

Cigarette butts were the most common debris found on U.S. shores during 1997's International Coastal Cleanup. Not syringes or tampon applicators, if you can believe it.

**After flirting with
a cute store clerk, realize you
had a slight string of snot
stretching from your
nose to your ear**

OR

**that after playing with your
dog earlier, you had a tiny spot
of poop on your cheek?**

If that slight string of snot is green or
yellower than usual, you're sick. Those
colors come from bacteria and their
waste. And if that dog poop has green
plastic in it, the mutt's been eating
out of the garbage again.

Accidentally run over and kill your best friend's cat with your car

OR

be forced to eat a small poodle that you never met?

BROILED POODLE

The simplest way to cook a dog, if it is young and tender, is to broil it. Skin the pooch, draw it, and split it. Rub well with salt, freshly ground pepper, and a bit of dried sage or thyme. Butter well, place on a broiling rack, and broil about 4 inches from the heat, allowing about 12–14 minutes per side for a 10- to 15-pound dog. Brush with butter during the broiling process, and turn once or twice before finishing off. Serve with home-fried potatoes, hot biscuits, and currant jelly. A beet and endive salad will balance the meal nicely.

IN 1987 A CREW OF THE SOUTH CAROLINA HIGHWAY DEPARTMENT PAINTED A YELLOW STRIP ACROSS A DEAD CAT LYING IN THE ROAD. MEE-OOWWWW!

Eat three earthworms

OR

wear a necklace made of them on your wedding day?

POETRY 101 MEETS WORMS 101: AN ESSAY

The late poet Richard Brautigan wrote *The Purple Worm Jewelry of North Carolina*. He also wrote *An Unfortunate Woman*, a perfectly titled work about any bride who wears a necklace of earthworms. Brautigan also wrote *Trout Fishing in America*, which is a far better use of earthworms. His *The Octopus Frontier* is reminiscent of our own (unpublished) *An Ode to the Eight-Legged Worm*. Brautigan's *Revenge of the Lawn* suggests what happens when worms go bad. And the "perverse" part of his *Willard and His Bowling Trophies: A Perverse Mystery* perfectly sums up this essay. The end.

After three days without eating,
have a sumptuous
Thanksgiving meal
placed in front of you
and win $5,000 by waiting
16 hours to eat it

OR

just dig in?

Percentage of
average guys
who'd rather
marry a great
cook than a
sexual dynamo:
30%

A beggar walked up to
a well-dressed woman
shopping on Rodeo Drive
and said, "I haven't eaten
anything in four days."

She looked at him and
said, "God, I wish I had
your willpower."

Lick the tongue of a random dog for thirty seconds

OR

steal a bone from a pit bull?

THE *KAMA SUTRA*, THE CLASSICAL INDIAN TEXT ON EROTICISM, DESCRIBES TWENTY KINDS OF KISSES, BUT NONE WITH DOGS.

As for stealing from a pit bull, that's "bone," not "boner," right? Because that would make one hell of a big difference.

Q. What do you get when you cross Lassie with a pit bull?

A. A dog that bites off your leg and then runs for help.

Drink water from a vase containing two-week-old dead flowers

OR

eat a giant three-foot-by-three-foot spiderweb?

WHEN A BUG GETS TRAPPED IN A SPIDER'S WEB, THE SPIDER FIRST BITES IT TO INJECT IT WITH PARALYZING POISON, THEN THROWS UP ACID ALL OVER IT TO BREAK IT DOWN AND MAKE IT EASIER TO EAT.

SPIDERS' "SILK" IS STRONGER THAN STEEL THREADS OF THE SAME DIAMETER.

A shot of vodka or gin poured into the water for cut flowers helps them to stand up straight rather than sag.

Have to hang onto the top of a car going 100 mph for ten minutes

OR

try to stay on the top of a hot-air balloon in the sky for ten minutes?

Fear of this new hanging-on-to-hot-air-balloons-and-fast-cars scenario is known as anemoneoochothanatoillyngoasthenobaroacrotraumatocatapeda-anablemetalloaeroacrohodophobia.

Because:
anemophobia is fear of wind
neophobia is fear of anything new
ochophobia is fear of a moving automobile
thanatophobia is fear of death
illyngophobia is fear of dizziness when looking down
asthenophobia is fear of fainting
barophobia is fear of gravity
acrophobia is fear of heights
traumatophobia is fear of injury
catapedaphobia is fear of jumping from high and low places
anablephobia is fear of looking up
metallophobia is fear of metal
aeroacrophobia is fear of open high places
hodophobia is fear of road travel

Drink the water from the hot tub after a fraternity party

OR

drink Mexican tap water?

Legionnaire's disease, tuberculosis, and herpes germs have all been found in hot tubs. However, the most common bacterial infection contracted in hot tubs results in an untreatable red, itchy rash that lasts for about ten days. The rash is often accompanied by a sore throat, sore eyes, chills, fever, nausea, and cramps.

IN MEXICO, DRINK BOTTLED WATER ONLY, DON'T SING IN THE SHOWER, DON'T BRUSH YOUR TEETH WITH TAP WATER—AND IF YOU'RE STUCK, BOIL WATER FOR FORTY MINUTES AND ADD EIGHT DROPS OF IODINE PER GALLON OF WATER BEFORE DRINKING IT.

Be known for your bad habit
of sniffing people's armpits
whenever you greet them

OR

be known for scooping
after your dog with your
bare hands instead of using
a pooper scooper?

At the Odor Clinic in Boston, deodorants
are tested by heating up humans and then
having other humans smell their armpits.
"The job isn't so bad . . . most of the time.
You might hear an occasional 'Whoa!'"
admits Brian Rogers, who works in the
company's Toiletries Technology Lab.

Pee in your pants
at your wedding
(in front of everyone)

OR

not be able to stop laughing
at your grandmother's funeral?

UPSIDE

The wedding pee is a surefire $10,000 winner on one of
those funniest-videos-ever TV shows, and that's going to
pay for a terrific honeymoon.

OPTIONS

Gatling's Funeral Home in Chicago offers a drive-through
service so that you can laugh your ass off while viewing
your grandmother through what's essentially the teller
window.

Laugh when you should cry and cry when you should laugh

OR

never be able to do either?

AN AVERAGE PERSON LAUGHS ABOUT 15 TIMES A DAY.

When Abraham Lincoln was asked how he felt after losing an election, he said he felt like a little boy who had stubbed his toe in the dark—too old to cry but in too much pain to laugh.

"HE WHO LAUGHS, LASTS."

—Mary Pettibone Poole

As a man, have to lick sugar off an extremely obese woman's inner arm rash

lap up maple syrup from her linty belly button?

COUNTRY SONG TITLES QUIZ

Which two did we make up?

a. "Drop Kick Me, Jesus, Through the Goalposts of Life"
b. "Get Your Biscuits in the Oven and Your Buns in the Bed"
c. "Get Your Tongue Outta My Belly Button 'Cause I'm Kissing You Goodbye"
d. "Her Teeth Were Stained, But Her Heart Was Pure"
e. "How Can I Miss You if You Won't Go Away?"
f. "I Don't Know Whether to Kill Myself or Go Bowling"
g. "I Fell in a Pile of You and Got Love All Over Me"
h. "I Licked Her and She Kicked My Butt"
i. "I'm Just a Bug on the Windshield of Life"
j. "I'm the Only Hell Mama Ever Raised"
k. "If Love Were Oil, I'd Be a Quart Low"
l. "If You Don't Leave Me Alone, I'll Go and Find Someone Else Who Will"
m. "My Wife Ran Off with My Best Friend, and I Sure Do Miss Him"
n. "Pardon Me, I've Got Someone to Kill"
o. "She Got the Ring and I Got the Finger"

Answers: c and h

Thoroughly lick a large frog all over

OR

just once, lick a two-inch area of the back side of the urinal in a Port-a-Potty?

THE LICKABLE FROG

Frogs must close their eyes to swallow.

Some North American tree frogs pee before jumping; that way they weigh less and can jump farther.

If you're ever near Eureka Springs, Arkansas, be sure to check out Frog Fantasies. You'll find over 6,000 frog-shape things to lick: spoons, pipes, toys, salt shakers, etc. A public rest room is offered for further licking.

THE LICKABLE TOILET

About a third of Americans flush while still sitting on the toilet.

The key to inventing an indoor toilet that didn't stink was putting a bend in the disposal pipe that blocked sewer odors.

If you're traveling in New England, be sure to check out the American Sanitary Plumbing Museum in Worcester, Massachusetts. You'll find yourself in the midst of a fascinating presentation of old toilets, catalogs, bathtubs, urinals, sinks, tools, and books—all of which you can lick when nobody's looking.

Eat a small cactus

OR

a cup of pebbles?

According to *The Wall Street Journal*, medical researchers are conducting clinical trials of a tiny camera that a patient swallows. "The camera travels into the small intestine, flashing two pictures every second. About 50,000 photos are transmitted to a special belt worn by the patient, and the information is later downloaded into a computer. After its journey, the camera is passed unnoticed by the patient and can be flushed down the toilet." The article goes on to compare the camera's size to "a large vitamin," "a marble," and "a pebble." But *not* a cactus!

As a woman, have quadruplets

OR

have four babies, all 10 months apart?

"If nature had arranged that husbands and wives
should have children alternatively,
there would never be more than three in a family."
—LAURENCE HOUSMAN

"We all worry about the population explosion,
but we don't worry about it at the right time."
—ARTHUR HOPPE

"If men could get pregnant,
abortion would be a sacrament."
—FLORYNCE KENNEDY

Eat a small can of cat food

OR

seven lemons
(seeds, pulp, juice, and rind)?

THE INGREDIENTS OF 9-LIVES
TUNA & OCEAN WHITEFISH ENTRÉE

Tuna, water, pea fiber, whitefish, calcium carbonate, soybean oil, choline chloride, vitamin supplements, zinc sulfate, sodium nitrite, thiamine mononitrate, niacin, manganese sulfate, riboflavin supplement, calcium pantothenate, pyridoxine hydrochloride, biotin, folic acid, potassium iodide

THE INGREDIENTS OF SEVEN LEMONS

Lemons

Always speak in rhyme

OR

not hear every third word spoken to you?

ROSES ARE ___
VIOLETS ARE ___
SAY THIS ___
AND WIN ___

Have to eat five peach pits

OR

half a pound of watermelon seeds?

ALMONDS ARE
MEMBERS OF
THE PEACH FAMILY.

"Watermelon—
it's a good fruit.
You eat, you drink,
you wash your face."
—ENRICO CARUSO

Always be tired

OR

always be tense?

"THE AMOUNT OF SLEEP REQUIRED BY THE AVERAGE PERSON IS ABOUT FIVE MINUTES MORE."

—Max Kauffmann

A guy walks into a doctor's office.

"Doc," the guy says, "I think I'm a tepee. And then I think I'm a wigwam. Then a tepee. Then a wigwam. And so on and so on. What's wrong with me?"

"Your problem is that you're two tents."

(Two tents. Too tense. Get it?)

Turn back the clock and be able to say or do one thing you never got to say or do

OR

take back one thing you said or did?

On average, it cost $80,000 to rehabilitate a seal after Alaska's *Exxon Valdez* oil spill. At a triumphant and emotional ceremony, two of these costly animals were released into the water amid cheers and applause from onlookers. A minute later, in full view, they were both eaten by a killer whale.

Swallow
a live goldfish
without water

swallow
a teaspoonful
of cold fish eyes?

If that goldfish is pregnant, it's a twit. That's right, *twit* is the official term for a pregnant goldfish.

FISH DON'T HAVE EYELIDS. THAT'S WHY THEY SLEEP WITH THEIR EYES OPEN— THEY HAVE TO.

A GOLDFISH HAS A MEMORY SPAN OF THREE SECONDS.

Eat an uncooked but thawed TV dinner

OR

a can of cold beef chili?

The following is an actual instruction label on Swanson frozen dinners:
Serving suggestion: Defrost.

If you like frozen food and are possibly a little paranoid, consider living in igloo country. An igloo will stand up to modern artillery better than a concrete barricade. In addition, it is almost invisible from the air and can't be spotted by infrared sensors.

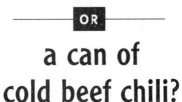

HUMANS PASS BETWEEN 1 CUP AND 1 GALLON OF GAS EACH DAY.

Have double vision

hear a constant echo?

A DUCK'S QUACK DOESN'T ECHO, AND NO ONE KNOWS WHY.

"I SEE THREE BASEBALLS, BUT I ONLY SWING AT THE MIDDLE ONE."

—Paul Waner, major league outfielder, on how he managed to hit successfully after drinking sprees

Be surrounded
by dozens of sharks

OR

have only one shark nearby,
with no risk of more arriving,
but while you are bleeding?

STATISTICALLY SPEAKING, IT IS MORE
LIKELY THAT YOU'LL BE KILLED BY . . .
A PIG,
A COW,
LIGHTNING, OR
A BEE
. . . THAN A SHARK.

A shark can
detect one
part of blood
in 100 million
parts of water.

Live in a home without electricity

OR

a home without running water?

In 1891, the White House lights were always on, night and day. President Benjamin Harrison and his family were terrified of the newly installed electricity and refused to touch the switches.

But they were OK with the White House plumbing. No problem there. The Harrisons happily touched faucets, Hot and Cold knobs, spigots. . . . You name the pipe and they'd touch it.

As a young man on a sinking ship when there is one space left on the last lifeboat, give it to a man in his late 70s

OR

take it yourself?

Believe it or not, some viewers of *Gilligan's Island* took the show seriously. The U.S. Coast Guard received several telegrams from concerned citizens asking why they didn't rescue the *Minnow*'s crew.

Suck pea soup from a biker's beard

OR

eat baby drool while the little tike is eating strained peas?

POGONOPHOBIA: FEAR OF BEARDS

A MAN FILED FOR DIVORCE FROM HIS WIFE IN HONOLULU, HAWAII, BECAUSE SHE "SERVED PEA SOUP FOR BREAKFAST AND DINNER . . . AND PACKED HIS LUNCH WITH PEA SANDWICHES."

What's the difference between roast beef and pea soup?

Anyone can roast beef.

Chew the beak off a chicken

OR

bite the legs off half a dozen mice?

TO MAKE THE SOUND OF THOUSANDS OF RATS IN *INDIANA JONES AND THE LAST CRUSADE*, THE SOUND OF CHICKENS CLUCKING WAS PLAYED AT HIGH SPEED.

In the Arctic, people regularly enjoy a dish called Mice in Cream. Mice are first soaked in ethyl alcohol (whoa!), fried in imported pork fat, then sautéed in more ethyl alcohol with some garlic, and topped off with a dollop of cream.

As a young adult, investigate your family tree and find out there is a lot of insanity in your family that hits people when they reach middle age

OR

find that no one has lived past 65?

If you are unable to comprehend the difference between right and wrong, you might qualify as legally insane. You can test yourself with the standard "M'Naghten Test" (established in 1843). The American judicial system recognizes 24 forms of insanity or incompetence, all of which may relieve a person from criminal responsibility to varying degrees, depending on the case.

The chance that a U.S. adult under the age of 54 suffers from mental-health and/or substance-abuse problems is 1 in 3.

Thoroughly lick
the entire surface of
ten one-dollar bills and
two dollars' worth of quarters

OR

thoroughly lick
the mouthpieces
of four football players
after a game?

IT TAKES ABOUT
142 LICKS TO
REACH THE
CENTER OF A
TOOTSIE POP.

Approximately
three hundred
$10,000 bills
are in circulation
in the U.S.

Suck fresh milk directly from the udder of a cow

OR

drink store-bought milk two days after it's "gone bad"?

What do you call a cow who can't give milk?
An udder failure.

What do you say about store-bought milk that robs a bank?
It's gone bad.

Get caught by your boss masturbating in your favorite superhero outfit

OR

screwing his/her spouse?

IN MICHIGAN IT'S AGAINST THE LAW
TO PUT A SKUNK IN YOUR BOSS'S DESK,
BUT IT'S NOT AGAINST THE LAW FOR THAT
BOSS TO CATCH YOU BEATING OFF AS THE
INCREDIBLE HULK. SO THAT'S GOOD.

Teenage comic book writers
Jerry Siegel and Joseph Shuster
got screwed when they sold all
rights to their superhero
character, Superman, for $130.
So that's *not* good.

Eat a steak that's been left
on a busy freeway for an hour
(it's probably very tender)

OR

drink a glass of wine that has
been slowly sifted through
the hairpiece of a sweaty
fat man with dandruff?

A HAIKU BY URKOV

**Both options replete
With methyl-ethyl bad stuff
Dripping from within**

—Michael Urkov, Redding, CA

Speaking of hairpieces, on May 20, 1997, Marv Albert
denied all charges that he committed assault and
forcible sodomy against a 41-year-old female friend.
Charges stated that he bit the woman as many as
15 times and forced her to perform oral sex.

Drink a two-ounce glass of liquid from a huge blister

OR

eat a salad covered with "Bits O' Scabs"?

FIBRINOGEN, ONE OF THE CONNECTIVE PROTEINS THAT MAKE UP SCABS, LOOKS JUST LIKE SILLY STRING WHEN VIEWED UNDER A MICROSCOPE.

DOCTORS RECOMMEND THAT YOU NOT POP BLISTERS. HOWEVER, IF YOU'RE REALLY THIRSTY AND YOU CAN'T RESIST, USE A SHARP SEWING NEEDLE BUT DO *NOT* HEAT THE NEEDLE OVER AN OPEN FLAME FIRST (THE HEATED NEEDLE CAN LEAVE A CARBON DEPOSIT IN YOUR SKIN).

Marry someone who is kind but not really in love with you

OR

marry someone who treats everyone else terribly and disrespectfully but totally adores you?

How would the world be different if people didn't get married?

"There sure would be a lot of kids to explain, wouldn't there?"
Kevin, 8

"You can be sure of one thing—the boys would come chasing after us just the same as they do now."
Roberta, 7

A husband and wife had a bitter quarrel on the day of their 40th wedding anniversary.

The husband yelled, "When you die, I'm getting you a headstone that reads 'Here Lies My Wife—Cold As Ever.'"

"Oh yeah?!" she replied. "When you die, I'm getting you a headstone that reads, 'Here Lies My Husband—Stiff At Last.'"

Eat poison ivy

OR

a handful of bumblebees?

A LITTLE RULE TO
REMEMBER WHEN EATING
PLANTS IN THE FOREST:
"LEAVES OF THREE,
LET THEM BE."

The average number of times a U.S.
beekeeper is stung each year: 400

Never have people take you seriously

OR

always have people think you are no fun?

THE ROLLER COASTER WAS INVENTED SO
THAT RUSSIA'S CATHERINE THE GREAT
COULD ENJOY THE THRILL OF HER
ELABORATE ICE SLIDES ALL YEAR LONG.

TED STRIKER: Surely you can't be
serious.

RUMACK: I am serious, and don't
call me Shirley.

—FROM *AIRPLANE!* (1980)

Lick the inside of a used toilet plunger

OR

the inside of a football player's jockstrap?

EVANGELISTA TORRICELLI, AN ITALIAN PHYSICIST AND MATHEMATICIAN WHO LIVED FROM 1608 TO 1647, IS RECOGNIZED AS FATHER OF THE TOILET PLUNGER. TORRICELLI WAS THE FIRST TO FIGURE OUT THAT THERE IS SUCH A THING AS A VACUUM—SPACE IN WHICH NOTHING EXISTS. THIS EVENTUALLY LED TO THE DEVELOPMENT OF MANY OF OUR MOST FAVORITE THINGS, LIKE THE RUBBER DART, THE VACUUM CLEANER, AND, YES, THE TOILET PLUNGER.

"When the child is twelve, your wife buys her a splendidly silly article of clothing called a training bra. To train *what*? I never had a training *jock*."
—BILL COSBY

Have to suck all the ink out of a ballpoint pen

OR

paint your tongue with Wite-Out®?

"I KNOW YOU HAVE A CIVIL TONGUE IN YOUR HEAD. I SEWED IT IN THERE MYSELF."

—from *I Was a Teenage Frankenstein*

On average, 100 people choke to death on ballpoint pens every year.

Become allergic to all your favorite foods

OR

all animals?

Contrary to popular belief, pet allergies aren't caused by pets' fur, but by the allergens in their saliva, urine, and dander (which are all carried on the fur).

LOTS OF PEOPLE HAVE BAD REACTIONS TO PARTICULAR FOODS, BUT ONLY 2% OF ADULTS AND 5% OF CHILDREN SUFFER FROM REAL FOOD ALLERGIES.

Be unable to stand up for yourself

OR

never know when to back down?

You could always borrow someone else's defense system . . . Sea slugs swallow the stinger cells of jellyfish. The cells then get digested and make their way to the sea slug's skin, where the slug uses them as if they were its own.

In Oakland, California, SWAT teams spent two hours in a standoff with a gunman who had barricaded himself inside his home. After launching ten tear gas canisters, officers discovered that the man was standing beside them, shouting to "please come out!" and give himself up.

For the rest of your life,
eat your least favorite
foods hygienically
prepared

OR

eat your favorite foods
prepared in
risky circumstances?

**Top three most hated foods in the U.S.:
tofu, liver, and yogurt**

Have a fat, nasty ass

OR

floppy jowls?

The "big butt" look was so popular in Europe throughout the 1700s that women wore pillowish fake ones under their dresses.

SOME OF THE SAME FOLKS HAD LOST THEIR TEETH AND USED "PLUMPERS"—CORK BALLS PLACED INSIDE THE CHEEKS TO PUFF THEM OUT.

Drink a glass of water out of a storm drain

OR

drink a large puddle left on the bathroom floor after someone gets out of the shower?

IN THE SHOWER,
75% OF PEOPLE WASH
FROM TOP TO BOTTOM.

Dibble is the official word
for drinking like a duck
(lifting the head after each sip).

Be a millionaire and then hit rock bottom

OR

live your entire life with just enough money to get by?

A CITIBANK SURVEY ON U.S. DIVORCE RATES FOUND THAT MONEY PROBLEMS WERE LISTED AS THE CAUSE IN OVER FIFTY PERCENT OF DIVORCES.

Over one million people became millionaires in 1999, and 250,000 more did so in the first quarter of 2000. By the end of 2000 the slide was on: 80,000 people had lost their newfound millionaire status.

Find inside a cake bought from a bakery a wad of bloody gauze

OR

a piece of a broken hypodermic needle?

Certain disease-producing bacteria die when subjected to an oven heat treatment; other bacteria grow hard-ass spores that protect the baby bacteria inside them. In the latter case, you need more extreme measures—higher temperatures and chemical treatment—to rupture these spores and kill the deadly infantile bacteria.

So forget rationalization. Go for opportunity. Do a thorough vomit, cross your fingers, get a good attorney, and retire very wealthy.

Eat a bottle cap

OR

a spider the size of a bottle cap?

In the Amazon, the Kayap people are such adventurous eaters that their language has more than 100 different words for diarrhea.

SAM MALONE'S GOOD LUCK CHARM IN TV'S *CHEERS* WAS A BOTTLE CAP.

Pee out of your nose

OR

poop out of your ear?

Poop is made up of undigested food, water, skin cells, bacteria, salts, bacteria poop, and pigment.

Some people's pee turns red after they eat lots of beets, and some people's pee stinks after they eat asparagus.

OSTRICHES PEE ON THEIR LEGS TO COOL DOWN.

Drink a gallon of used hot dog water

OR

a shot glass of someone else's foot sweat?

The feet have more sweat glands than any other part of the body.

ROMAN (DAN AYKROYD):
HOW ABOUT THE GOURMET HERE, YOU KNOW WHAT HE WANTED, HOT DOGS. YOU KNOW WHAT THEY MAKE THOSE THINGS OUT OF, HUH CHET, HUH? LIPS AND ASSHOLES!
—from *The Great Outdoors*

The intestines of sheep, pigs, and oxen are what holds hot dogs together.

Have food poisoning
and be forced to eat
what made you sick

OR

have to smell tequila during
a severe tequila hangover?

Wake up in the morning.
Put your feet on the floor.
Do the 50-yard dash to the bathroom door.
Diarrhea, diarrhea!

When you're sliding into first
And you feel something burst,
Diarrhea, diarrhea!

When you're sliding into third
And you lay a juicy turd,
Diarrhea, diarrhea!

When you're sliding into home
And you feel something foam,
Diarrhea, diarrhea!

DEAN WORMER:
FAT, DRUNK, AND
STUPID IS NO WAY
TO GO THROUGH
LIFE, SON.

-from *Animal House*
(1978)

Lick a melted chocolate bar off the sidewalk

OR

a friend's plush pile car seat, including all the crevices?

If there was chocolate on the car seat, the M&M/MARS Consumer Affairs Department in New Jersey (1-800-627-7852) does not recommend licking.

Instead, first remove all excess chocolate. Next spray area with Shout brand cleanser. Let that sit for 10 to 15 minutes. Then scrub with soap and water. If you don't have Shout, try most any dishwashing detergent. Again, let it soak in before scrubbing.

THE AVERAGE AMERICAN EATS TWELVE POUNDS OF CHOCOLATE A YEAR.

From the random file on "Melted Anything": Pearls dissolve in vinegar.

Lick all the bugs off an 18-wheeler's radiator after a long haul

OR

suck on frozen dog poop for 30 seconds?

THE DUNG BEETLE
EATS WHAT IT LIVES
IN—ANIMAL POOP.

A sampling of 414 flies found
an average of 1,250,000
bacteria on each one's body.

By your actions, project the message "I'm an easy mark"

OR

project "leave me alone"?

Easy mark?
Atlanta Braves pitcher John Smoltz was burned during 1990 spring training when he attempted to steam-iron a shirt while wearing it.

Leave me alone?
Pitcher Alejandro Pena refused a child's autograph request before a 1990 game because the child addressed him as "Mr. Jalapeno."

What's honeymoon salad?
Lettuce alone.

Eat one can of soft dog food

OR

five cups of dry dog food?

ALPO Prime Cuts Gourmet Dinner in Gravy (the ingredients)

Water, poultry, beef, wheat gluten, meat by-products, wheat flour, cornstarch, whole chicory root, salt, caramel color, potassium chloride, tricalcium phosphate, sodium tripolyphosphate, natural flavor, zinc sulfate, vitamin supplements (E, A, B12, D3), ferrous sulfate, thiamin mononitrate, copper sulfate, manganese sulfate, niacin, calcium pantothenate, riboflavin supplement, pyridoxine hydrochloride, potassium iodide, folic acid, sodium selenite, biotin

Purina Dog Chow (the ingredients)

Ground yellow corn, poultry by-product meal, corn gluten meal, soybean meal, beef tallow preserved with mixed tocopherols, brewers rice, dicalcium phosphate, calcium carbonate, malted barley flour, salt, dried whey, potassium chloride, L-lysine monohydrochloride, animal digest (Is that like *Reader's Digest*?), choline chloride, zinc oxide, ferrous sulfate, vitamin supplements, manganese sulfate, niacin, calcium pantothenate, brewers dried yeast, riboflavin supplement, biotin, garlic oil (Ah-ha! The secret to dog breath!), pyridoxine hydrochloride, copper sulfate, thiamine mononitrate, folic acid, menadione sodium bisulfite complex, calcium iodate

Be the dumbest person in high school

OR

the ugliest?

At age ninety, Peter Mustafic of Botovo, Yugoslavia, was suddenly no longer the dumbest guy in town—he began to speak again after a silence of 40 years. "I just didn't want to do military service, so I stopped speaking in 1920; then I got used to it."

(But just try not being ugly anymore.)

A man says to God: "God, why did you make my woman so beautiful?"

God says: "So you would love her."

"But God," the man says, "why did you make her so dumb?"

God says: "So she could love you."

Occasionally and intentionally treat people you care about like dirt

OR

occasionally and intentionally ignore them when they need you?

Dear Reyer School:

God bless you for the beautiful radio I won at your recent senior citizen's luncheon. I am 84 years old and live at the county home for the aged. All my people are gone. It's nice to know that someone thinks of me.

God bless you for your kindness to an old forgotten lady. My roommate is 95 and always had her own radio, but would never let me listen to it, no matter how often or sweetly I asked.

The other day her radio fell and broke into a lot of pieces. It was awful. She was very upset. She then asked if she could listen to mine, and I said "F%$# you!"

Sincerely,
Edna Johnston

Have kids who are very smart
but don't do well socially

OR

who are popular and engaging
but only C and D students?

KIDS' ADVICE TO KIDS

"Don't sneeze in front of your mom when you're eating crackers." *Michael, age 14*

"You can't hide a piece of broccoli in a glass of milk." *Elizabeth, age 9*

"Don't pick on your sister when she's holding a baseball bat." *Joey, age 9*

ONE NIGHT A LITTLE BOY'S PARENTS
OVERHEARD THIS PRAYER:
"NOW I LAY ME DOWN TO REST,
AND HOPE TO PASS TOMORROW'S TEST.
IF I SHOULD DIE BEFORE I WAKE,
THAT'S ONE LESS TEST I HAVE TO TAKE."

Go out with someone gorgeous
who flirts just enough that
people assume that he or she
must be cheating on you

OR

go out with someone only half
as good looking who rarely flirts
or arouses suspicion?

"He's the kind of man a woman would have to marry
to get rid of."
—MAE WEST

"What men call gallantry and gods adultery
Is much more common where the climate's sultry."
—LORD BYRON

"I've been married for 34 years, and I'm still in love with
the same woman. If my wife ever finds out, she'll kill me."
—HENNY YOUNGMAN

"Adolescence is the stage between infancy and adultery."
—UNKNOWN

Have to always eat standing up

OR

always enter your car from the passenger door?

RANDOM CAR STATISTICS

Number of American guys who lost their virginity in a car?
1 in 7

Number of times the average American guy has had sex in a car?
15

Car driven almost exclusively by men?
Porsche 911

Car driven almost exclusively by women?
VW Cabriolet

After a ten-mile run, have to drink a gallon of hot coffee

OR

a half gallon of cream?

You know when you've had too much coffee when:

You answer the door before people knock.

You grind your coffee beans in your mouth.

You can type 60 words per minute . . . with your feet.

You don't sweat, you percolate.

> "You have to stay in shape. My grandmother, she started walking five miles a day when she was 60. She's 97 today and we don't know where the hell she is."
>
> —ELLEN DEGENERES

Win a Nobel prize for an idea you stole

OR

become wealthy from an invention that hurts people?

ALBERT NOBEL (1833–1896) INVENTED DYNAMITE AND, BECAUSE OF IT, AMASSED A HUGE FORTUNE. HE LEFT MOST OF THAT FORTUNE TO ENDOW ANNUAL NOBEL PRIZES.

EVERY YEAR NEARLY 9,000 PEOPLE INJURE THEMSELVES WITH A TOOTHPICK.

Drink half a cup of a stranger's saliva

OR

eat all the hair out of your bathtub drain?

Just to rule one thing out, saliva is a very unlikely source for infection with HIV (human immunodeficiency virus, the microbe that causes AIDS). Although small amounts of HIV can be found in saliva—enough to test—so little virus is present that a human bite is not considered a significant risk for transmitting HIV.

DISEASE-CAUSING BACTERIA MOST OFTEN ENTER YOUR BODY THROUGH YOUR MOUTH.

Human hair grows an average of twenty-six feet in a lifetime.

Be marked with a tracking device so that the government always knows where you are

OR

with a microphone so that it always knows what you are saying?

"THERE'S ADAM CLYMER,
A MAJOR LEAGUE ASSHOLE
FROM THE *NEW YORK TIMES*."

—President George W. Bush, speaking
into a microphone without realizing it
was turned on

After death, choose to live the same life over again

OR

risk being reborn anywhere in the world in any circumstance?

SURPRISE!
We're not going to go with the obvious video recommendation (*Groundhog Day* with Bill Murray). Instead, try *12:01* with Jonathan Silverman (in his best work since *Weekend at Bernie's*).

After death, choose to live the same life over again

OR

risk being reborn anywhere in the world in any circumstance?

SURPRISE!
We're not going to go with the obvious video recommendation (*Groundhog Day* with Bill Murray). Instead, try *12:01* with Jonathan Silverman (in his best work since *Weekend at Bernie's*).

That was weird.

Have sex with someone with no arms

OR

no legs?

"IF YOU SEE ONE, IT'S PROBABLY MINE."

—Theresa Uchytil, Miss Iowa, pointing out to the other Miss America contestants that she sometimes leaves her prosthetic hand lying around

Be caught having an affair
with your best friend's spouse

OR

be caught with your child's
18-year-old best friend?

MOVIE RECOMMENDATION TIME!

In *Play It Again, Sam,* Woody Allen is having an affair with his best friend's spouse, Diane Keaton.

In *Class,* Jacqueline Bisset is having an affair with her teenage son's best friend, Andrew McCarthy.

A man comes home from work and finds his girlfriend packing her things. "Where are you going?" he asks.

"I'm leaving because everyone says you're a pedophile," she replies.

"Well, that's a mighty big word for a 10 year old!" he counters.

Be the reason
for an accident
that leaves
a stranger dead

OR

a friend
crippled?

ASK A KENNEDY.

Be lost where there are no street signs to point the way

OR

no people to ask?

So there are two cities ahead of you. In one city, *all* the people *always* tell the truth. In the other city, *all* the people *always* lie. You want to go to the truthful city. Suddenly, you come to an unmarked fork in the road. One road leads to the truthful city and one leads to the lying city. Standing at the fork is a resident of one of those cities, but you don't know which city. You are allowed to ask her only one question. What should you ask that will get you on the correct road to the truthful city?

Be sure to ask "Which road leads to the city you're from?" If she's from the truthful city, she'll point to the correct road. And if she's from the lying city, she'll point to the truthful city road. Bingo! You're as good as there.

Be made to lick 1,000 public telephone receivers

OR

eat a half cup of ear wax?

Ear wax comes in two different varieties—wet and dry. The type of wax that you have is determined by your heritage. Most white, black, and Hispanic people have wet wax, which is oily, sticky, and tan colored. Most Asian and Native American people have dry wax, which is sticky, brittle, and gray. OK?

Work as an accountant for John Gotti

OR

Manuel Noriega?

A TOUGH GUY JOKE

For years two brothers—one a lawyer and the other a deaf-mute accountant—worked for a mobster. Whenever the mobster and the accountant needed to communicate, the lawyer brother would use sign language and serve as interpreter.

One day the mobster realized his books were short three million dollars. He called in the two brothers. Looking at the lawyer and pointing to the accountant, he screamed, "You tell this son-of-a-bitch I want to know where my money is!"

The brothers conversed briefly, and the lawyer reported that his brother had no idea what the mobster was talking about.

Furious, the mobster put a gun to the accountant's head and screamed at the lawyer brother, "Tell this bastard that he lets me know—right now—where the money is or I'll blow his brains out!"

The lawyer conveyed this to his brother, who immediately explained—in frantic sign language—that the money was hidden in a suitcase under his basement steps.

"Well? What'd he say?" yelled the mobster.

The lawyer shrugged. "He says you don't have the balls."

Eat a sandwich bag full of lawn clippings

OR

eat one live earthworm?

"Whenever I watch TV and see those poor starving kids all over the world, I can't help but cry. I mean, I'd love to be skinny like that but not with all those flies and death and stuff."

—MARIAH CAREY

Knowing full well that
the charges are without merit,
be accused in the tabloids
of cross-dressing

OR

of sleeping with
an underaged person
of the opposite sex?

"I can do anything. In *GQ*,
I appeared as a man."

—BOY GEORGE

"DO YOU THINK
INFANTS HAVE
AS MUCH FUN
IN INFANCY AS
ADULTS HAVE
IN ADULTERY?"

—Anonymous

THE LAST YEAR
THAT IT WAS
LEGAL TO MARRY
A 14-YEAR-OLD
IN UTAH WAS
1999.

WOULD YOU RATHER...

Be ruled exclusively by your heart

OR

exclusively by your mind?

Love	vs.	*Think*
I love you.		I think you.
Linda Lovelace.		Linda Thinklace.
Virginia is for lovers.		Virginia is for thinkers.
All you need is love.		All you need are thoughts.
I love New York.		I think New York.
Lover's Lane.`		Thinker's Lane.
Courtney Love.`		Courtney Think.
Love is never having to say you're sorry.		Thinking is never having to say you're sorry.
Love at first sight.		Thought at first sight.
Love conquers all.		Thoughts conquer all.
How do I love thee? Let me count the ways.		How do I think thee? Let me count the ways.

"It is a joy for me to have a son who has inherited the main trait of my personality: the ability to rise above mere existence by sacrificing oneself through the years for an impersonal goal. This is the best, indeed the only way in which we can make ourselves independent from personal fate and from other human beings."

—ALBERT EINSTEIN, CONGRATULATING HIS SON HANS ALBERT—WHOSE BIRTHDAY ALBERT NEVER REMEMBERED—FOR BEING JUST LIKE HIMSELF WHEN IT CAME TO PLACING WORK OVER FAMILY

Have someone throw a scuba tank into the middle of the ocean, then have to wait 10 seconds, dive in, and try to retrieve it so you don't drown

have someone throw a parachute out of a plane, after which you must also wait 10 seconds before diving after it to avoid splatting?

Leonardo da Vinci designed a parachute that didn't allow air to pass through its top. So instead of falling straight, the chute tilted to the side, out went the air, and BOOM-SPLAT!! The guy should've just stuck to painting pretty pictures of his girlfriends.

THE BEACH BOYS, WHO WERE CONSIDERED THE KINGS OF CALIFORNIA SURFING, STARTED A NATIONAL SURFING CRAZE IN THE EARLY 1960S. FOUR OF THE ORIGINAL MEMBERS OF THE BAND KNEW NOTHING ABOUT SURFING, AND THE ONLY ONE WHO DID DROWNED IN 1983.

Be forever homeless but free to roam the earth

OR

live the life of luxury in a mansion that you could never leave?

"I'VE BEEN RICH
AND I'VE BEEN
POOR. BELIEVE
ME, HONEY,
RICH IS BETTER."
—Sophie Tucker

GERMAN POLICE
KEEP ARRESTING
A HOMELESS MAN
WHO COOKS OVER
BERLIN'S "ETERNAL
FLAME." THE GUY'S
ESPECIALLY FOND OF
COOKING DUMPLINGS
AND ONION SOUP.

Have your breath smell like a bad fart

OR

have your laugh sound like a fart?

In one true incident, a horrid diet and poor ventilation were pinned as the cause of death for a man found dead in his nearly airtight bedroom. It appeared that the man—suffering from excessive gas brought on by his consumption of beans and cabbage exclusively—died in his sleep from methane gas inhalation.

Three of his rescuers got sick and one was hospitalized.

WOULD YOU RATHER...

Have the power to read minds

OR

have the power to make anyone fall in love with you?

HOW DO YOU DECIDE WHOM TO MARRY?

"You got to find somebody who likes the same stuff. Like if you like sports, she should like it that you like sports, and she should keep the chips and dip coming." *Alan, age 10*

"No person really decides before they grow up who they're going to marry. God decides it all way before, and you get to find out later who you're stuck with." *Kirstin, age 10*

WHEN IS IT OKAY TO KISS SOMEONE?

"When they're rich." *Pam, age 7*

Oh! . . . to be in love! Did you know that 15% of U.S. women say they have sent flowers to themselves on Valentine's Day?

Always wear shoes that are a half size too small

OR

always have your underwear creeping up your butt?

MEN'S HAT SIZES IN THE UNITED STATES ARE ALWAYS OFF 5/32 OF AN INCH. IT SEEMS THAT THE TOOLMAKER WHO MADE THE FIRST "HAT-SIZING DEVICE" GOOFED.

THE GOOD NEWS IS THAT THEY DIDN'T PUT THE SAME GUY IN CHARGE OF SHOES.

The maximum portion of buttocks that one can legally bare in public in Manatee County, Florida, is 2/3.

ACCORDING TO A GARMENT INDUSTRY STUDY, 75% OF WOMEN WEAR THE WRONG SIZE BRA.

In one sitting, eat ten pounds of cheese

OR

a bucket of peanut butter (with nothing to drink)?

EACH YEAR, AMERICANS
EAT 6 MILLION POUNDS
OF SQUEEZE CHEESE.

Arachibutyphobia
is the fear that
peanut butter will
stick to the roof of
your mouth.

Be extremely lucky

OR

extremely smart? (but not both)

In the 19th century, the British Navy decided to dispel the superstition that Friday was an unlucky day. The keel of a new ship was laid on a Friday, she was named H.M.S. *Friday*, commanded by a Captain Friday, and finally went to sea on a Friday. Neither the ship nor her crew were ever heard of again.

George Schwartz, the owner of a factory in Providence, Rhode Island, barely survived a 1983 blast that totaled his factory except for one wall. After being treated for minor injuries, he returned to the scene to see what he could salvage. The remaining wall promptly collapsed on him and killed him.

"I deserve respect for the things I did not do."
—DAN QUAYLE

Have intense sinus pressure

OR

chronic constipation?

APPROXIMATELY 35 MILLION AMERICANS SUFFER FROM CHRONIC SINUSITIS.

APPROXIMATELY 4.5 MILLION AMERICANS SUFFER FROM CHRONIC CONSTIPATION.

In 1966, Thomas J. Bayard invented a vibrating toilet seat. Bayard maintained that physical stimulation of the buttocks could help sufferers to relieve their constipation.

Be caught picking your nose on the huge screen at a big stadium

OR

on a first date with someone special?

ASK 100 PEOPLE AND 70 WILL ADMIT
TO PICKING THEIR NOSES. THREE OF
THOSE 70 WILL ADMIT TO EATING WHAT
THEY FIND. AND TO THINK THESE
PEOPLE DATE AND GO TO BALL GAMES.

Be stranded at sea on a small rowboat with only one flare

OR

with only one paddle?

ACCORDING TO THE *WORST-CASE SCENARIO SURVIVAL HANDBOOK* (CHRONICLE BOOKS, 1999), THE THING TO DO WHEN A SHARK ATTACKS IS TO HIT IT WITH QUICK, SHARP, REPEATED JABS IN THE EYEBALLS.

Have your nipple ring yanked out

OR

have to lift 20 pounds with your nose ring?

Lorne Green
(*Bonanza*'s Ben Cartwright)
had one of his nipples bitten off
by an alligator while hosting
Lorne Green's Wild Kingdom.
"Wild" is right!

As a 25 year old, forget your entire childhood to age 15

OR

lose your memory of the last five years?

The doctor tells his patient: "Well, I have good news and bad news . . ."

The patient says, "Lay it on me, Doc. What's the bad news?"

"You have Alzheimer's disease."

"Good heavens! What's the good news?"

"You can go home and forget about it!"

Discover that your perfect match (soul mate) is someone other than the person you've married and get to meet him or her

OR

marry someone you love but never meet your perfect match (soul mate) at all?

IS IT BETTER TO BE SINGLE OR MARRIED?

"It's better for girls to be single but not for boys. Boys need someone to clean up after them." *Anita, age 9*

The ratio of husbands who say they fell in love with their spouse at first sight to wives who say this: 2 to 1

"Single is better, for the simple reason that I wouldn't want to change no diapers. Of course, if I did get married, I'd just phone my mother and have her come over for some coffee and diaper-changing." *Kirsten, age 10*

If you had to do it all again, have parents who partied too much and had no morals

OR

were militantly strict and always went by the book?

YOU MAKE THE CHOICE!

Strict parents

Party parents

Must salute Dad when he drops you off at school.

Mom gets your date high, Dad screws her.

Your math teacher's frightened of Mom.

Your math teacher's sleeping with Mom.

Make a mistake and you have to do 50 push-ups and 100 sit-ups.

Make a mistake and you have to buy smokes and lottery tickets for the folks.

Dinner: steak, potatoes, green beans, and tossed salad.

Dinner: hash brownies.

Must wash and wax car and fill gas tank before using.

First night out with the new driver's license and you get pulled over; turns out the folks' car is hot.

Eat a shot glass full of live wasps

OR

eat a shot glass?

In 1951, 17-month-old Mark Bennet was stung 447 times by wasps and lived. A shot glass was not involved.

OF THE STINGS RESULTING FROM A SHOT GLASS FULL OF WASPS, HORNETS, YELLOW JACKETS, OR HONEYBEES, THE WORST WOULD BE THE HORNETS.

Be so intelligent that no one can relate to you

OR

be as dumb as a brick but likable?

"She dumped me 'cause she said I wasn't paying enough attention to her, or something. I don't know, I wasn't really listening."

—HARRY DUNNE, *DUMB & DUMBER*

This moron goes running over to his friend's house all excited that he completed a jigsaw puzzle. Beaming with pride, he announces that he completed the puzzle in five months. His friend says, "What's so great about that?" The moron says, "Are you kidding? The box says three to seven years!"

"CONSEQUENCES FOR THE CONSTITUTION OF RADIATION FOLLOWING FROM THE ENERGY DISTRIBUTION LAW OF BLACK BODIES."

—Albert Einstein, title of early paper

Have to lie motionless while a fruit bat licks fruit jelly off your face

OR

while a vulture eats roadkill off your stomach?

WHEN THE INDIAN FRUIT BAT (SO NAMED BECAUSE IT LIKES FRUIT JELLY?) OF SOUTHEAST ASIA SPREADS ITS WINGS, THEY MEASURE FIVE FEET FROM TIP TO TIP.

To prevent infection while standing in the rotting animals they eat, vultures poop on their own feet. (The poop contains antibiotics.) And remember, vultures are bald because they shove their heads into places where feathers would get messy.

Suck the white dried spit
off the edges of
a speaker's lips
after a two-hour talk

suck the crud that gathers in
the corner of a cat's eye?

What is that crud that gathers
in the corner of the cat's eye?

And why is the word
abbreviation so long?

And if a man says something in the
woods and no woman is there to hear,
is he still wrong?

Be stupid and rich

OR

smart and poor?

AT&T fired President John Walter because he lacked "intellectual leadership." The fool received a $26 million severance package.

"I WANT A MAN WHO'S KIND AND UNDERSTANDING. IS THAT TOO MUCH TO ASK OF A MILLIONAIRE?"

—Zsa Zsa Gabor

As an adopted woman,
find out that your real father
is a serial killer

OR

that you once dated him
for a month when
you were in your twenties?

"PARENTS ARE THE LAST
PEOPLE ON EARTH WHO
OUGHT TO HAVE CHILDREN."
—SAMUEL BUTLER

In Pittsburgh, city councilman
Otis Lyons refused to support
abortion in cases of incest
because "some of the great
leaders in the Bible married
their sisters."

Chew shards of broken glass

OR

sit on a lighted barbecue grill?

When a list of the ten most-grilled foods was compiled, neither broken glass nor your butt made the cut. If only it had been the twenty most-grilled foods. . . .

1. steak
2. chicken
3. hamburgers
4. hot dogs
5. pork chops
6. ribs
7. bratwurst/sausage
8. potatoes
9. corn
10. fish

Have body odor that can be detected across the yard

OR

be hairy like Bigfoot?

Years ago, physicians were more likely to smell you. For example, if your doctor sniffed your sweaty skin and caught the smell of stale beer and freshly baked brown bread, you were likely to have tuberculosis and typhoid. Or if he smelled you from across the yard, you were likely to need a shower.

IT IS ESTIMATED THAT THERE HAVE BEEN 1,500 "WELL-DOCUMENTED" SIGHTINGS OF BIGFOOT SINCE 1958.

Goose bumps are reminders that humans were once covered with hair. Which was really handy. When we were cold, the hair stood on end to create a trap for air and provide a layer of insulation. When we were threatened, the hair stood up to make us look a lot bigger than we really were. (Dogs still do that.) Although all that hair is long gone, our skin still "bristles" in both situations.

Only be able to tell lies

OR

have to scream out every true thought that crosses your mind?

WHAT DO MOST PEOPLE DO ON A DATE?

"On the first date, they just tell each other lies, and that usually gets them interested enough to go for a second date." *Mike, age 10*

"WHAT KIND OF A MICKEY MOUSE OPERATION ARE WE GETTING INTO HERE?"

—angry Disney World executive to representatives of troubled Delta Airlines (with which Disney had recently entered into a business partnership)

Drink liquid found leaking from a garbage bag

OR

chew on a hairy substance found between the cushions of your couch?

AFTER DROPPING OUT OF INDIANA UNIVERSITY, LARRY BIRD ATTEMPTED TO CLEAN UP HIS ACT BY TAKING A JOB AS A GARBAGE COLLECTOR.

VISIT THE HAIR MUSEUM IN INDEPENDENCE, MISSOURI, WHICH FEATURES WEIRD THINGS MADE OUT OF HUMAN HAIR. A HAIRCUT IS INCLUDED IN THE ADMISSION PRICE.

Be left at the altar

have your spouse leave a month after the wedding?

Wow, this suggests an idea for a "reality TV" special. Like you'd get this supposed millionaire guy. Then you'd have all these strange women who promise to marry him if he chooses her as a bride. Then you'd have this contest on TV. Then the guy and the winning woman would get married on live TV. Then they'd go off on a honeymoon. Then she'd leave him right after the honeymoon. Then he'd turn out not to really be a millionaire. And she'd end up posing nude in a girlie magazine. And then—nah! Forget it! Nothing like that would ever happen.

A woman gets home, screeches her car into the driveway, runs into the house, slams the door, and shouts at the top of her lungs, "Honey, pack your bags. I won the damn lottery!"

The husband says, "Ohmigod! No way! What should I pack, beach stuff or mountain stuff?"

The wife yells back, "It doesn't matter . . . just get the hell out!!"

Knowing you will die tomorrow, spend your last night drinking with your friends

OR

having sex with your favorite movie star?

IN 1980, A LAS VEGAS HOSPITAL HAD TO SUSPEND SEVERAL OF ITS EMPLOYEES FOR BETTING ON WHEN PATIENTS WOULD DIE.

A passenger jet was being knocked around by a severe thunderstorm. A white-knuckled young woman turned to the priest sitting beside her and with a nervous laugh asked, "Father, you're a man of God, can't you do something about this storm?"

He looked at her and replied, "Lady, I'm in sales, not management."

Be considered annoying

OR

dull?

From an actual employee performance evaluation in a large U.S. corporation:

"If you see two people talking and one looks bored . . . he's the other one."

As a man, have to tell your wife that you cheated on her once while you were dating

OR

have to tell your wife that her wedding ring is fake?

Three men died and went to heaven. Upon their arrival, St. Peter asked the first if he had been faithful to his wife. The man admitted to two affairs during his marriage. St. Peter told him that he would receive only a compact car to drive in heaven.

Then St. Peter asked the second man if he had been faithful to his wife and the man admitted to one affair. St. Peter told him he would be given a midsize car to drive.

The third man was asked about his faithfulness, and he told St. Peter he had been true to his wife until the day he died. St. Peter praised him and gave him a luxury car.

A week later the three men were driving around, and they all stopped at a red light. The men in the compact and midsize cars turned to see the man in the luxury car crying. They asked him what could possibly be the matter—after all, he was driving a luxury car.

"I just passed my wife," he told them, "and she was on a skateboard."

"Honesty has ruined more marriages than infidelity."
—CHARLES MCCABE

Live until you are 80 and die after six months of unbearable pain that can't be helped with drugs

OR

live to 55 and die peacefully?

FAMOUS LAST WORDS

"THIS WALLPAPER IS KILLING ME; ONE OF US HAS GOT TO GO."
—Oscar Wilde, playwright

"WHY SHOULD I TALK TO YOU? I'VE JUST BEEN TALKING TO YOUR BOSS."
—Wilson Mizner, Hollywood impresario, to an attendant priest

"WHY, YES—A BULLET-PROOF VEST."
—James Rodgers, a murderer before the firing squad, when asked if he had a final request

Cheat on your spouse and have nobody know

OR

not cheat and have everyone think you did?

"WOMEN MIGHT BE ABLE TO FAKE ORGASMS,
BUT MEN CAN FAKE WHOLE RELATIONSHIPS."
—Sharon Stone

"HONESTY IS THE KEY TO A RELATIONSHIP.
IF YOU CAN FAKE THAT, YOU'RE IN."
—Courtney Cox (as Monica on *Friends*)

"THERE IS ONE THING I WOULD BREAK UP
OVER AND THAT IS IF SHE CAUGHT ME
WITH ANOTHER WOMAN.
I WOULDN'T STAND FOR THAT."
—Steve Martin

Shave your mom's bikini line

OR

your dad's butt?

The bikini was invented by designer Louis Reard in 1946.

Your dad's butt didn't have to be invented. It just showed up, years ago.

Have a mother who is a well-known prostitute

OR

a mother only you know is a murderess?

VIDEO RENTAL MOMENT!

Dixie: Changing Habits
A New Orleans madam and a mother superior go head to head before all ends well—(Hey, it's Hollywood!)—with nuns paying off debts and prostitutes cleaning up their lives.

Murder-in-Law
Graphic slasher flick about a mother-in-law who escapes from an insane asylum—(Hey, it's Hollywood!)—and terrorizes her son-in-law's family in a series of gruesome killings.

Be able to change three incidents in the past

OR

alter three future situations?

> "HISTORY WILL BE KIND TO ME
> FOR I INTEND TO WRITE IT."
> —Winston Churchill

FIVE WAYS TO PREDICT THE FUTURE

1. alectromancy: studying how a chicken picks up grain

2. geoloscopy: listening to the way a person laughs

3. myomancy: watching the movements of mice

4. molosophy: feeling the moles on a person's body

5. bibliomancy: reading random passages in a book

Get a glimpse, while still living, of heaven

OR

hell?

"What! You been keeping records on me? I wasn't so bad! How many times did I take the Lord's name in vain? One million and six? Jesus Chr—!"

—STEVE MARTIN

"Hell is other people."
—JEAN PAUL SARTRE

Feed your children by regurgitation

OR

have to lick them to bathe them?

"Kids are without a doubt the most suspicious diners in the world. They will eat mud (raw or baked), rocks, paste, crayons, ball-point pens, moving goldfish, cigarette butts, and cat food. Try to coax a little beef stew (or barf) into their mouths and they look at you like a puppy when you stand over him with the Sunday paper rolled up."

—ERMA BOMBECK

"IT WOULDN'T HURT A BABY IF IT NEVER HAD A BATH."

—British physicians Drs. Margaret Kerr and Gavin C. Arnell

Eat a handful of chicken feathers

OR

five tablespoons of frog eggs?

Olympic badminton rules say that the birdie has to have exactly fourteen feathers.

THE LONGEST RECORDED FLIGHT OF A CHICKEN IS THIRTEEN SECONDS.

The female Australian brooding frog lays eggs so the male can fertilize them. She then eats the fertilized eggs and gives birth to little "froglets" by vomiting them up five weeks later.

Have a house
with no roof

have a house
with no walls
(like a carport)?

Or the wrong house?

In November 2000 it was discovered that the roofed and walled house of Shakespeare's mother, Mary Arden, visited by over 100,000 people a year, was actually the wrong house.

The Shakespeare Birthplace Trust will have to relocate the designation to another farmhouse 20 yards away. As for the thousands of photos taken by happy visitors since 1930, well, never mind.

Be too naïve

OR

too cynical?

"I was so naïve as a
kid, I used to sneak
behind the barn and
do nothing."
—JOHNNY CARSON

"NO MATTER HOW CYNICAL
I GET, I JUST CAN'T KEEP UP."
—Lily Tomlin

See the SWAT team pull up to your home

OR

the HAZMAT (hazardous materials) team?

To request your FBI file (those SWAT guys must be there for some reason!), send a note requesting your file to:

Director
Federal Bureau of Investigation
Washington, DC 20535

Your note should read something like: *"Pursuant to the Freedom of Information Act, Title 5, United States Code, Section 552, I hereby request access to. . . ."* Then ask for specific info, like organizations, schools, jobs, etc.

Meanwhile, Washington, D.C., has the most lawyers and New Jersey has the most toxic-waste dumps because New Jersey had first choice.

In your 12-year-old child's room, find a box of condoms

OR

a bottle of "uppers"?

TY: You take drugs, Danny?

DANNY: Every day.

TY: Then what's your problem?

—Caddyshack

THE RAMSES BRAND CONDOM
IS NAMED AFTER THE GREAT
PHARAOH RAMSES II, WHO
FATHERED MORE THAN
160 CHILDREN.

Be an alcoholic

OR

a kleptomaniac?

THE FINGERPRINTS OF A KOALA ARE VIRTUALLY INDISTINGUISHABLE FROM THOSE OF HUMANS—SO MUCH SO THAT THE TWO COULD BE CONFUSED AT A CRIME SCENE.

"He resolved, having done it once, never to move his eyeballs again."

—KINGSLEY AMIS, ON RECOVERING FROM A HANGOVER

Always be itchy

OR

always feel like you have to pee?

Years ago, it was thought that an itchy thumb promised that you would soon have a visitor.

Nowadays, it is thought that always feeling like you have to pee promises that the bathroom will soon have a visitor.

GROUNDS FOR DIVORCE?

In Lynch Heights, Delaware, a woman filed for divorce because her husband "regularly put itching powder in her underwear when she wasn't looking."

Fall in love with someone
who has done hard time
in prison for a triple murder

OR

with someone who is
a member of
a bizarre religious cult?

In 1924, Pep, the dog that killed Pennsylvania
governor Pinchot's cat, was sentenced to life
imprisonment at the state penitentiary.

THE LARGEST CULT MURDER-SUICIDE OF OUR
TIME TOOK PLACE ON NOVEMBER 18, 1978,
IN JONESTOWN, GUYANA. LED BY THE
REVEREND JIM JONES, THE 914 MEMBERS OF THE
PEOPLE'S TEMPLE CULT COMMITTED SUICIDE BY
DRINKING CYANIDE-LACED PUNCH. PARENTS
FED THE POISON TO THEIR CHILDREN.

Not be able to tell the time

not know left from right?

AMERICANS ARE MOST LIKELY TO HAVE SEX AT 10:34 P.M.

As a man, have your wife artificially inseminated by your best friend

OR

your brother?

Erection is chiefly caused by scuraum, eringoes, cresses, crymon, parsnips, artichokes, turnips, asparagus, candied ginger, acorns bruised to powder and drunk in muscadet, scallion, and sea shellfish.

—ARISTOTLE,
4TH CENTURY B.C.

President Jimmy Carter's brother was Billy. A beer was named after him.

Pick up a hitchhiker on a deserted highway

let a vagrant stay overnight in your house?

Percentage of average men who would pick up a hitchhiking . . .

Hot, twentysomething girl wearing jean shorts: 61%
Pregnant woman: 23%
Priest: 6%
Stephen Hawking: 6%
Elderly man: 4%

On any given night, more than 700,000 Americans will not have shelter. More than two million Americans will be homeless at some point each year.

Have others watch a video of you on the toilet

OR

a video of you throwing a childish temper tantrum?

During the late 1600s in France, it was considered a great honor to speak with King Louis XIV while he sat on the pot relieving himself.

"DOES IT SHOW?"

—Richard Kelly,
U.S. Congressman, after stuffing $25,000 in cash into his pocket while secretly being videotaped by the FBI

While running through the woods from an enraged wild boar, sprain your ankle severely

accidentally step into an old metal bucket and not be able to shake it off as you run?

A BOAR JOKE

Two guys were walking through the woods when they came upon an enraged wild boar.

The first guy quickly sat down, took off his dress shoes, and put on sneakers.

"Why do that?" yelled the second guy. "You can't outrun that wild boar!"

"I only have to outrun you," said the first, as he took off at full speed.

Save all your photo albums from a house fire

OR

save the family dog?

"A photograph never grows old. You and I change, people change all through the months and years but a photograph always remains the same. How nice to look at a photograph of mother or father taken many years ago. You see them as you remember them. That is why I think a photograph can be kind."

—ALBERT EINSTEIN

Meanwhile, according to *USA Today*, 17% of all Americans would throw their pets off a cliff for $1 million.

AVERAGE NUMBER OF STRUCTURES THAT CATCH FIRE IN THE U.S. EACH HOUR: 60

Have the kind of personality that causes people to believe you are a conniving manipulator

OR

a pathological liar?

"I'M NOT GOING TO HAVE SOME REPORTERS PAWING THROUGH OUR PAPERS. WE ARE THE PRESIDENT."

—Hillary Clinton, commenting on the release of subpoenaed documents

SAM: "Don't worry about it, Woody. I'm sure everyone will forgive you."

WOODY: "But it was a lie, Sam, and I've never told a lie before. No wait, that's a lie. See, now that's two lies. See how much easier it gets. [starts to get hysterical and cry] Oh my God, I'm out of control. What's next, *murder*?"

—FROM *CHEERS*

Know when your spouse is going to die and have to tell him or her

OR

know when you're going to die and not be able to tell your spouse?

"My girlfriend's weird. One day she asked me, 'If you could know how and when you were going to die, would you want to know?' I said, 'No.' She said, 'Okay, forget it.'"

—STEVEN WRIGHT

Have no skin sensations
(be completely numb to touch)

OR

have super-hypersensitive skin
that feels everything
ten times more intensely?

Speaking of medical conditions, these are some actual medical interview tidbits collected from reports taken by paramedics, emergency room receptionists, and (unfortunately) doctors, all at major hospitals:

- "The patient stated that she had been constipated for most of her life until 1989 when she got a divorce."

- "Bleeding started in the patient's rectal area and continued all the way to Los Angeles."

- "Both of the patient's breasts are equal and reactive to light and accommodation."

Fill a large pail with beach sand using only your mouth

OR

chew and swallow one pound of raw seaweed or kelp?

ONE OF THE . . .

. . . things found in the lungs of those who drown at the beach is sand.

. . . ingredients in ice cream is seaweed.

Have your spouse find out about three affairs you had while engaged

OR

about one affair you had while married?

THINK "HILLARY RODHAM."
THINK "HILLARY CLINTON."

"MY WIFE HAS CUT OUR LOVEMAKING DOWN TO ONCE A MONTH, BUT I KNOW TWO GUYS SHE'S CUT OUT ENTIRELY."

—Rodney Dangerfield

Vote for an honest but stupid politician

OR

a liar with tremendous savvy?

POST IMMEDIATELY

Due to an anticipated voter turnout much larger than originally expected, the polling facilities may not be able to handle the load all at once. Therefore, Democrats are requested to vote on Tuesday, November 7. The Republicans and Independents will vote on Wednesday, November 8. Please pass this message along and help us to make sure that nobody gets left out and everything will run smoothly with this minor change. Know where your polling place is!! Be sure to vote!!!
Presidential Election Commission

> "Politics is not a bad profession. If you succeed there are many rewards; if you disgrace yourself you can always write a book."
>
> —RONALD REAGAN

NEW ZEALAND WAS THE FIRST PLACE
IN THE WORLD TO ALLOW WOMEN TO VOTE.

Live in a country run by super models

OR

live in a country run by professional football players?

"IF I WEREN'T SO BEAUTIFUL MAYBE
I'D HAVE MORE CHARACTER."
—Jerry Hall, super model and Rolling Stones spouse

"I never set out to hurt anybody
deliberately . . . unless it was, you
know, important, like a league game
or something."
—DICK BUTKUS, PROFESSIONAL FOOTBALL PLAYER

Eat a dozen raw eggs, shell and all

OR

four raw potatoes?

In the 1985 election for
mayor of Boise, Idaho,
Mr. Potato Head
received four votes.

MERRIAM-WEBSTER'S
COLLEGIATE DICTIONARY
(10TH ED.) DEFINES EGG AS
"AN ANIMAL REPRODUCTIVE BODY."
EASY TO FORGET ABOUT THAT,
HUH?

*Potatoes will take food stains off your
fingers. Just slice and rub raw potato
on the stains and rinse with water.*

Be a compulsive liar

OR

marry one that you can't divorce?

"Judges lie, then lawyers lie, then clients lie."
—ALAN DERSHOWITZ (REPORTED OCTOBER 25, 1993)

"Lawyers don't lie."
—ALAN DERSHOWITZ (REPORTED DECEMBER 10, 1994)

"Why are lawyers thought of so badly?
Why are we found near the bottom of nearly
every public opinion ranking of occupations?
The answer is simple: Because we deserve it!"

—ALAN DERSHOWITZ
IN HIS BOOK *CONTRARY TO PUBLIC OPINION*

In a 40-yard sprint in which your life depends on victory and you forfeit if you start early, and having been told to start on "three" with no time for questions, use a count of 1, 2, 3, then GO

OR

1, 2, then start on 3?

The thing to do is fart on the count of one. Your opponents will get the giggles, and you'll be off on your way to victory. Works every time.

MARATHON RUNNERS OFTEN SUFFER FROM BLOODY NIPPLES, WHICH ARE CAUSED BY LONG, HOT RUNS IN WHICH SWEAT AND CHAFING RUB NIPPLES RAW.

Be trapped
in a room full
of enthusiastic preaching
televangelists for eight hours

OR

in a room full of raucous
circus clowns for
the same amount of time?

"Lord, if you want me to have that house in California you can help me make the payments just as you can help me make the payments on this one in Charlotte."
—REV. JIM BAKKER

God said to Pat Robertson (according to Pat Robertson), "Pat, I want you to have an RCA transmitter."
—PAT ROBERTSON

Give thanks that "in Thy sovereignty Thou hast permitted Richard Nixon to lead us at this momentous hour of our history."
—REV. BILLY GRAHAM

"Pledge at least $100! Borrow it if necessary!"
—REVEREND IKE

"Hi, kids!"
—RAUCOUS CIRCUS CLOWN

Be able to fly

OR

be able to become invisible?

Found on the label of a
child's Superman costume:
"Wearing of this garment
does not enable you to fly."
(The label that warns about
invisibility can't be seen.)

Did you know . . .
There's a Superman
reference in every
episode of Seinfeld.

WOULD YOU RATHER . . .

Come home and
have the feeling someone
has been in your apartment,
but nothing is missing

OR

have your apartment
obviously ransacked,
but nothing is missing?

A man went to the police station wishing to speak with the burglar who had broken into his house the night before.

"You'll get your chance in court," said the desk sergeant.

"No, no, no!" insisted the man. "I want to know how he got into the house without waking my wife. I've been trying to do that for years!"

Be caught walking nude on a beach by a policeman

OR

have your horn get stuck while your car is behind a gang of Hell's Angels?

Your car horn tends to stick? Then be sure to load up the glove compartment with acid. In 1964, poet Allen Ginsberg and the Hell's Angels' Sonny Barger shared some LSD and within hours they were chanting together.

A Tifton, Georgia, man has been convicted of public indecency and placed on probation for slinging chunks of lard at women while driving a car in the nude.
—Associated Press

Wake up unexpectedly in the hospital

OR

wake up unexpectedly in your neighborhood jail?

REGULATIONS OF PHILADELPHIA GENERAL HOSPITAL, 1790

Patients may not swear, curse, get drunk, behave rudely or indecently on pain of expulsion after the first admonition. There shall be no card playing or dicing and such patients as are able shall assist in nursing others, washing and ironing linen and cleaning the rooms and such other services as the matron may require.

CAMELOT! STARRING GORDON BENJAMIN!

Massachusetts inmate Gordon Benjamin turned down parole rather than miss the chance to play Lancelot in a prison production of *Camelot*.

Eat one live tarantula

OR

hold a live wasp in your mouth for one minute?

Wasps feed their offspring regurgitated caterpillar.

THOUGH NOT POISONOUS, EACH HAIR ON THE VERY HAIRY TARANTULA FUNCTIONS AS A SHARP DART WHEN THE CREATURE IS THREATENED.

Marry a whiner

OR

marry a bully?

"TILL I WAS 13,
I THOUGHT
MY NAME WAS
'SHUT UP.'"

—Joe Namath

In 1621, twelve women were sent from England to Virginia to be sold as wives. The price was 120 pounds of tobacco apiece, or approximately one pound of tobacco per pound of woman. Choosing a nonwhiner out of the bunch wasn't an option.

·Inherit a piece of land between two battling countries

OR

inherit a piece of land near an active volcano?

Long ago, the people of Nicaragua believed that if they threw beautiful young women into a volcano, it would stop erupting. So how's about throwing some beautiful young Nicaraguans into the middle of the Korean DMZ? Write your congressperson.

Eat a package of cookies for breakfast every day for a month

OR

drink 15 cups of coffee a day for a month?

"Chocolate chip cookies: half-sit, half on the bed, propped up by a pillow. Read a book. Place cookies next to you on the sheet so that crumbs get in the bed. As you eat the cookies, remove each chocolate chip and place it on your stomach. When all the cookies are consumed, eat the chips one by one, allowing two per page."

—DELIA EPHRON,
HOW TO EAT LIKE A CHILD

IN ONE YEAR, THE AVERAGE MAN CONSUMES 603 CUPS OF COFFEE.

IF YOU MANAGE TO CONSUME THE EQUIVALENT OF 70 TO 100 CUPS OF COFFEE IN ONE SITTING, YOU'LL EXPERIENCE CONVULSIONS AND MAY EVEN DIE.

Be very clumsy

very forgetful?

What wa—OUCH!—was the question?

WOULD YOU RATHER...

Get two weeks' paid vacation every year

OR

get six weeks' paid vacation a year but not be allowed to travel anywhere?

THE CLASSIC TWO-WEEK MUSEUM VACATION

Day	Museum (or hall of fame)	Location
Sunday	American Sanitary Plumbing Museum	Worcester, MA
Monday	Nut Museum	Old Lyme, CT
Tuesday	Lower East Side Tenement Museum	New York, NY
Wednesday	Center for the History of Foot Care	Philadelphia, PA
Thursday	Marvin Johnson's Gourd Museum	Fuquay-Varina, NC
Friday	The Museum of Dental History	Charleston, SC
Saturday	National Tick Museum	Statesboro, GA
Sunday	Frog Fantasies Museum	Eureka Springs, AR
Monday	Tooth Fairy Museum	Deerfield, IL
Tuesday	Dan Quayle Center and Museum	Huntington, IN
Wednesday	Museum of Questionable Medical Devices	Minneapolis, MN
Thursday	The Hair Museum	Independence, MO
Friday	Barbie Hall of Fame	Palo Alto, CA
Saturday	Burlesque Hall of Fame	Helendale, CA
Sunday	Cockroach Hall of Fame	Plano, TX

(fly home!)

Enthusiastically celebrate Thanksgiving on a daily basis

OR

New Year's Eve on a daily basis?

A FESTIVE HAIKU BY URKOV

If we had ice chest
    We could have some ice cold beer
    If we had some beer

—Michael Urkov, Redding, CA

Have all your wedding guests
come down with food poisoning

OR

have the father of your spouse
try to squeeze the fannies of all
of the female attendants?

Two schoolgirls eagerly offered to bake a cake for the
Estrella Mountain Elementary School carnival in Arizona.
The cake was to be a prize for one of the carnival events.
But instead of flour, eggs, and sugar the girls used dog
poop, pond water, and Ex-lax to make the cake. They then
smothered the baked cake in whipped cream and Snickers
bars. Something or someone alerted officials, and the
"delicacy" was confiscated before anyone ate any. The girls
were questioned and
threatened with a
charge of conspiracy
to commit assault.

"MARRIAGE HAS
DRIVEN MORE THAN
ONE MAN TO SEX."
—Peter De Vries

Be taken too seriously all the time

OR

be thought of only as a partyer?

The partyers are not always who you think they are. Facts about partying and partyers:

The average man with a college degree is 24 percent more likely to drink than a high-school dropout.

The number of casual sex encounters in which the average man or his partner has been drinking: 3 out of 5

The number of times the average man typically drives drunk (including multiple trips in one evening) before getting caught: 618

Be a freelance photographer on the front lines during a war

OR

a firefighter dropped behind the line in a raging forest fire?

URBAN LEGEND OPPORTUNITY

Firefighters in California recently found a corpse in a scorched area of forest while surveying the damage caused by a fire. The deceased male was wearing a wet suit, dive tank, flippers, and face mask. A coroner's inquiry revealed that the diver had died of massive internal injuries rather than burns. Investigators set about determining how a deep-sea diver ended up in the middle of a forest fire. Shockingly, they discovered that on the day of the fire, the individual was on a wreck dive off the coast—more than 20 miles from the forest. The firefighters, using advanced techniques to squelch the fire, had called in a phalanx of helicopters equipped with enormous buckets. The choppers flew to the ocean, filled the buckets with seawater, and returned to dump them on the fire. And . . . you guessed it. One minute our diver was making like Flipper in the Pacific, the next he was doing the breaststroke in a fire bucket 500 feet in the air. And then dumpo and BLAM!

Cause a car accident because you were staring at the butt of a sexy pedestrian

OR

have an uninsured driver hit you?

PERCENTAGE OF GUYS WHO THINK THEY'RE MUCH BETTER DRIVERS THAN THEIR WIVES OR GIRLFRIENDS: 92%

WHEN THE *WALL STREET JOURNAL* REPORTED ON LEGAL EFFORTS TO DEFINE THE TERM *BUTTHEAD*, THE TWO LEADING CANDIDATES WERE 1) "A WISE-CRACKING LOUT," AND 2) "AN ENDEARING, FUN-LOVING GUY."

Always look great to everyone
you meet but frequently
say the wrong thing

OR

always have the right thing to
say but frequently look terrible?

At the Miss America Pageant,
when Miss Delaware was
asked who her favorite
author was, she went with
Steven Spielberg.

"NO MATTER HOW GOOD
SHE LOOKS, SOME OTHER
GUY IS SICK AND TIRED
OF PUTTING UP WITH
HER SHIT."

—written on the men's room wall,
Linda's Bar and Grill, Chapel Hill,
North Carolina

Have a band of mariachi singers follow you everywhere

OR

have one determined bagpipe player follow you everywhere?

THE BAGPIPE WAS ORIGINALLY MADE FROM THE WHOLE SKIN OF A DEAD SHEEP. BUT MARIACHI SINGERS HAVE NEVER BEEN MADE OF DEAD MEXICANS.

Carnegie Mellon University (Pittsburgh) offers bagpiping as a major. Now there's a "roommate from hell" situation.

Have a social phobia that will never again allow you to hug or kiss anyone

OR

have a social phobia that will never again allow you to look a person directly in the eye?

THERE'S A WOMAN IN YORK, ENGLAND, WHO'S ALLERGIC TO PEOPLE. WHEN SHE KISSES HER HUSBAND, FOR EXAMPLE, THE AREA AROUND HER LIPS GETS SCRATCHY AND SPLOTCHY.

What percentage of public high school teachers favor banning students from kissing and hugging on school grounds: 69%

Bite the head off a live gopher

OR

thoroughly lick a cat's butt?

OR WORSE YET:
FREEZE A GOPHER AND LIGHT A BUTT?

Janitors at Fowler Elementary School in Ceres, California, cornered a gopher and sprayed it with several canisters of the stuff used to remove gum from the school's floors. Figuring they had "frozen the rodent to death," the janitors paused for a victory smoke.

BOOM! The solvent ignited, the janitors got blown out of the room, and 15 students were injured. (The gopher survived and was last seen running across a field.)

Have your identical twin be far more successful than you financially

OR

romantically?

Shortly after the death of his parents, Conrad Middleton, 26 years old, was killed by his twin brother, Brian, after a disagreement over who should inherit the family home. Conrad had a sinus condition that left him without a sense of smell. After a heated scuffle, Brian stormed out of the house, then sneaked back in and turned on the oven, filling the house with gas. He then left out a box of cigars, a lighter, and a note saying, "Sorry for the spree, have a puff on me, Brian." Conrad promptly lit a cigar, blowing up the house—and himself.

If your life depended on victory, have to run a 100-yard race against a 6th grader

 OR

against your own 11-year-old-dog?

HAIKUS BY URKOV

Is it easier
    To tackle a twelve year old
        Than a Labrador?

Many years training
    Instruction, classes, books, schools
        Will your choice come, sit?

—Michael Urkov, Redding, CA

THE HEAVIEST DOG ON RECORD WAS A ST. BERNARD THAT WEIGHED 310 POUNDS.

Have to apologize on national television for a marital infidelity

OR

for a sexual shortcoming?

In 1873, Reverend Henry Ward Beecher was charged with adultery. He escaped the suit on a legal technicality and thereafter drew larger crowds than ever—particularly when preaching on sin.

PERCENTAGE OF MEN WHO ADMIT THAT THEY'D RATHER LOSE THEIR WIVES OR GIRLFRIENDS THAN LOSE THEIR CARS: **14**

When Viagra first came out in 1998, French restaurateur Jean-Louis Galland decided to offer the substance as an ingredient in an exclusive recipe for consenting adults. M. Galland used one-fifth of a 50 milligram pill in each serving, until government inspectors confiscated his stash and forced him to stop dispensing drugs without a license.

Be an "ugly duckling"
until you graduate from college
and then blossom into
the proverbial swan

OR

be just a little better
than average looking
throughout your life?

Percentage of
Americans who
want to change
their bodies
in some way:
75%

Percentage of
Americans who
want to change
their intelligence:
13%

CONSIDER THIS.
IF YOU'RE A MALE,
NONE OF THIS
MAKES ANY
DIFFERENCE. OTHER
GUYS ALWAYS GET
THE GOOD-LOOKING
WOMEN ANYWAY.

Run a mile on a six-inch-deep bed of potatoes

OR

swim a quarter mile through maple syrup twelve feet deep?

DID YOU KNOW THAT 60% OF ALL UNITED STATES POTATO PRODUCTS ORIGINATE IN IDAHO?

A breaststroke race from Santa Monica to Catalina was held for female swimmers, and a brunette, a redhead, and a blonde were the competitors. After about 14 hours, the brunette staggered up onto shore and was declared the fastest breaststroker. About 40 minutes later, the redhead crawled in for second place. Nearly 4 hours after that, the blonde finally came ashore and promptly collapsed in front of the worried onlookers.

When the reporters asked why it took her so long to complete the race, she replied, "I don't want to sound like a sore loser, but I think those other girls were using their arms."

Top freestyle swimmers achieve a speed of only 4 miles per hour. (Fish, in contrast, have been clocked at 68 mph.)

Marry someone you can't beat at anything

OR

someone you beat at everything, without even trying very hard?

Have you tried "Strip *Zobmondo!!*"?

"A HUSBAND IS WHAT'S LEFT OF THE LOVER ONCE THE NERVE HAS BEEN EXTRACTED."
—Helen Rowland

Surprise your wife at work and find she's in a miniskirt and fishnet stockings she wasn't wearing when she left home

OR

surprise your husband at work and find out that he's got a hostile, gorgeous secretary he never mentioned?

In 1989 a Tel Aviv dentist, using a pseudonym and a call-girl agency, arranged for a prostitute. When he showed up at the designated motel room, the prostitute turned out to be his wife. It's assumed that they never got around to talking about any secretaries.

Percentage who said in 1994 that they would allow their spouse to have sex with a stranger in exchange for $1 million: 10%

Have to remove tied-together
sneakers that were thrown
over high-power lines
30 feet above you

OR

have to do enough research
to find the best explanation
for why people throw shoes
up there in the first place?

In 1832, Wait Webster
received a patent for
attaching rubber to
shoes, thereby inventing
something that in future
years could be thrown
over power lines 30 feet
above you.

MEANWHILE,
40% OF ALL
WOMEN ADMIT
TO HAVING
THROWN SHOES
AT MEN.

If your life depended on it,
have to keep a hula hoop
going for five minutes
without stopping

OR

have to pogo-stick
for 100 yards
without stopping or falling?

IN 1987,
ROXANN ROSE
HULA-HOOPED
FOR 90 HOURS.

In 1997,
Ashrita Furman
pogo-sticked
a distance of
23.11 miles.
It took twelve-
and-a-half hours.

Struggle through a dense crowd as a person who is only two feet tall

OR

as a person who has an enormous bulging belly?

Count Joseph Boruwlaski, a dwarf who was under three feet in height and entertained European royalty in the 1800s, married an actress of normal size. When she was angry with her husband, she would place him on the mantel.

IN 1987, AMERICAN WALTER HUDSON HAD THE WORLD'S LARGEST WAIST, MEASURING 9 FEET, 11 INCHES.

Have socially reclusive kids

OR

kids who are angry bullies?

"One of the disadvantages of having children is that they eventually get old enough to give you presents they make at school."

—ROBERT BYRNE

"NEVER RAISE YOUR HAND TO YOUR CHILDREN— IT LEAVES YOUR MIDSECTION UNPROTECTED."

—ROBERT ORBEN

ONE IN FOUR AMERICAN PARENTS BELIEVES THAT TEENAGERS ARE USUALLY "LIVELY AND FUN TO BE AROUND."

Be thought of as a bumbling, incompetent fool by everyone you work with

OR

as sexually inadequate by everyone you slept with?

Official Winner of the Bad Sex Award

Now. Yes. He rises, turns her over, flips her white body. Her small white body. She is so small and so compact, and yet she has all the necessary features. Shall I compare thee to a Sony Walkman, thou are more compact. She is his own Toshiba, his dinky little JVC, his sweet Aiwa. "Aiwa," she says as he enters her, "Aiwa, aiwa aiwa aiwa aiwa aiwa aiwa aiwa aiwa aiwa aiwaaaaaaaaahhh."

—FROM THE NOVEL
KISSING ENGLAND,
BY SEAN THOMAS

"I can't wear a pink shirt to work. Everybody wears white shirts. I'm not popular enough to be different."

—HOMER SIMPSON

If your parents were divorced, see your dad marry someone your age

OR

30 years his senior?

DISPATCHES FROM THE DIVORCE FRONT

- In 1982, 97-year-old Simon Stern of Wisconsin sought a divorce from his 91-year-old wife, Ida, because "she just isn't fun anymore."

- Impotence is grounds for divorce in 24 states.

- Men who say they are happier after their divorce: 58%.

- Women who say they are happier after their divorce: 85%.

- A man in Idaho was granted a divorce because his wife dressed up as a ghost and scared the man's mother away.

In a fight, be armed with only a Ping-Pong paddle

OR

a Wiffle bat?

David Mullaney's son and a friend liked to play stickball with a plastic golf ball. Mullaney figured that a ball that didn't roll or bounce as far as a rubber one had some value in the sporting world, so he began to experiment. He cut holes into a ball and played with it. Soon he noticed that if you put the holes in the right place, even the wimpiest thrower could toss that thing around like a pro. So in 1955, Mullaney started making and selling Wiffle balls (the name from the baseball term "to whiff," which means to strike out). The game became so popular that early in the next century, *wiffle* showed up in a *Zobmondo* question and everybody knew what it meant.

Be given a rectal exam by a dentist

OR

have a cavity filled by a proctologist?

In Leeds, England, 26-year-old store clerk Walter Hallas was so afraid of dentists that in 1979 he asked a coworker to cure his toothache by punching him in the jaw. The punch knocked Hallas off his feet to the floor, where he cracked his skull and soon died from the injury.

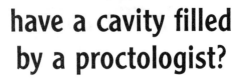

A DOCTOR GOES TO CASH A CHECK AT HIS LOCAL GROCERY STORE, AND PULLS A RECTAL THERMOMETER OUT OF HIS POCKET TO SIGN THE CHECK. QUITE EMBARRASSED, HE SAYS, "WELL, NOW THAT'S JUST GREAT! SOME A**HOLE HAS MY PEN."

As a woman, discover that your boyfriend has been making calls to three other women

OR

to a 976 phone-sex number?

In 1999, a 40-year-old female phone-sex operator won a workers' compensation settlement against Fort Lauderdale's CFP Enterprises, Inc. She claimed she developed carpal tunnel syndrome in both hands from masturbating up to seven times a day while speaking with callers. The amount of the settlement was not disclosed.

EITHER WAY, CHECK THE WEATHER CHANNEL BECAUSE RESOLUTION MAY SOON BE ON THE WAY—60% OF ELECTROCUTIONS OCCUR WHILE TALKING ON THE PHONE DURING A THUNDERSTORM.

Be stuck beside someone with horrific body odor on a crowded subway car for ten stops

OR

against someone who has an obvious erection on a long elevator ride?

Everybody has his or her own, individual odor. Bloodhounds can distinguish between any two people except identical twins (whose scents differ only if they've been eating very different foods for quite a while). We wonder, then, if it's worse for a bloodhound than for a person to be stuck beside someone with horrific body odor.

WHAT IS THE NUMBER OF SECONDS THAT THE AVERAGE AMERICAN CAN WAIT FOR AN ELEVATOR BEFORE BECOMING VISIBLY AGITATED? 40 SECONDS

"Hey, you! Brazilian jeweler guy! *Off the Elevator!*"

In 2000 a Brazilian jeweler, under medical supervision, used a special device to extend his smallish 4-inch penis to a whopping 10.5 inches. The stretch took over three years and is the longest ever achieved using the special traction tool.

Experience the *Titanic*

OR

the *Hindenburg?*

In 1898 (14 years prior to the *Titanic* tragedy), Morgan Robertson wrote *Futility,* a novel about the largest ship ever built hitting an iceberg in the Atlantic Ocean on a cold April night. The ship was named *Titan.* One publisher rejected the manuscript, saying that it was absurd to imagine a ship that large sinking.

"OH, THE HUMANITY!"

—newscaster, during live coverage of the *Hindenburg* explosion

Eat someone's tumor right after it has been extracted by surgery

OR

chew and swallow someone's eyeballs?

It pays to know your tumors before deciding. For example, the largest tumor ever was an ovarian cyst weighing 328 pounds taken from a woman in Texas in 1905. (She made a full recovery.)

"I believe that if ever I had to practice cannibalism, I might manage if there were enough tarragon around."

—JAMES BEARD

Live in a world where nobody cleans up after his dog

OR

everybody, including you, has to do it bare-handed?

Before 1880, when the Scott brothers started making what we'd consider toilet paper, people wiped themselves with leaves, corn cobs, the Sears, Roebuck catalogue, and when necessary, their hands.

"ALWAYS LOOK OUT FOR NUMBER ONE AND BE CAREFUL NOT TO STEP IN NUMBER TWO."

—Rodney Dangerfield

If your life depended on it, have to try to take apart and then reassemble a computer

OR

a car engine?

An auto mechanic received a repair order that said to check for a clunking noise when going around corners. He took the car out for a test drive and made a right turn, then a left turn, each time hearing a loud clunk.

Back at the shop, he returned the car to the service manager with this note:

"Removed bowling ball from trunk."

Eat a head of rotten cabbage

OR

drink a glass of sour milk?

First, confirm the details.

For example, in 1989, Bernard Lavery of Wales grew a 124-pound head of cabbage. Yet the federal government considers a glass of milk to be only eight ounces.

Live to be 100 years old

OR

start life over from birth and live to be only 60 years old, knowing what you know now?

IF YOU COULD LIVE FOREVER, WOULD YOU AND WHY?

"I would not live forever, because we should not live forever, because if we were supposed to live forever, then we would live forever, but we cannot live forever, which is why I would not live forever." (Miss Alabama in the 1994 Miss USA pageant)

ONE PERSON IN TWO BILLION WILL LIVE TO BE 116 OR OLDER.

Have a sleepwalking problem that causes you to wander the streets at night

OR

causes you to get up at night and pee all over your furniture?

While sleepwalking, an 11-year-old Illinois boy left his home, hopped a train, and was later found walking 100 miles from home.

Restoration experts discovered that the discoloration near the base of the Statue of Liberty was caused by its patina being worn away by laborers peeing from the top of the statue.

Eat 16 ounces of coffee skin (the film on top after the cup has been left out for two days)

OR

two gallons of beer foam?

AN ARCHAIC LAW ALLOWS THAT A SAUDI WOMAN CAN BE GRANTED A DIVORCE IF HER HUSBAND FAILS TO PROVIDE HER WITH COFFEE.

A man in La Vergne, Tennessee, called 911 to report that he and his wife were fighting and he needed the police to come to his house and stop her from pouring out all his beer.

Beer foam will subside if you rub your finger along your nose or rotate it in your ear canal, then stick it in the beer.

Wake up in the morning after
a drunken night and inexplicably
find blood all over yourself and
all over your bed

OR

find your .38 pistol,
usually stored in a closet,
next to you on the nightstand
with two bullets missing?

According to the *Wall Street Journal*, every
TV executive's favorite proposal for the
2000–2001 season was *Quantum Drunk*.
Described as "man wakes up each morning
drunk, and has to figure out what happened
the previous night." No network dared
produce it. Damn!

In a fit of anger and
frustration, curse someone
who cut in line
in front of you at a
movie for his or her race

OR

sexual preference?

According to a Kinsey Report . . .

Half the men raised on farms have
had a sexual encounter with an
animal.

White women, in particular those with
a college degree, are the most
receptive to anal sex.

Find out that while drunk
the night before,
you flashed the elderly woman
who lives next door

OR

that you pounded the hell out of
your own car with a hammer?

A man returned to his sports car to find a
freshly dented fender and this note under the
windshield wiper: "The people who saw me hit
your fender are now watching me write this
note, and probably figure I'm giving you my
name and phone number so you can contact me
and send me the bill. You should live so long!"

ACCORDING TO THE *NEW YORK TIMES*,
DOZENS OF RURAL AMERICANS ARE
KILLED EVERY YEAR AFTER THEY DRINK
TOO MUCH, LIE DOWN IN THE MIDDLE OF
THE HIGHWAY, AND GET RUN OVER.

Get caught masturbating by your mother

OR

catch your mother masturbating?

"When the habit is discovered, it must in young children be put a stop to by such means as tying the hands, strapping the knees together with a pad between them, or some mechanical plan."

—FROM *CRADLE TO SCHOOL, A BOOK FOR MOTHERS* (1902)

"If God didn't want us to masturbate he would've made our arms shorter."
—GEORGE CARLIN

Shortly after his parents split up, young Bobby passed by his mom's room and saw her rubbing herself and groaning, "I need a man, I need a man!" Over the next few months, he saw her doing this several times. Then he came home from school one day and heard her groaning again. When he peeked into her bedroom, he saw a man on top of her.

So Bobby ran into his room, took off his clothes, threw himself on his bed, and started stroking himself, moaning, "Ohhh, I need a bike, I need a bike!"

Live in a neighborhood
where your house is by far
the nicest and produces
"neighbor envy"

OR

where your house is
the ugliest and most run-down?

WHEN RESIDENTIAL UNITS IN BOSTON'S
REALLY UGLY PRUDENTIAL BUILDING
FIRST WENT ON SALE, MANY OF THE
BUYERS WERE WEALTHY BOSTONIANS
WHO FIGURED IT WAS BETTER TO LIVE
THERE AND LOOK OUT THAN TO LIVE
WHERE THEY MIGHT HAVE TO LOOK AT IT.

In a crowded movie theater, sit behind three very tall people

OR

in front of a group of loud giggling people?

MOVIE THEATER MAYHEM!

To create the language of the mutants in the 1932 film *Island of Lost Souls*, a mixture of animal sounds and foreign languages was recorded, then played back at alternating speeds. The sound caused audiences to vomit.

In the early 1960s, a movie called *Scent of Mystery* was accompanied by odors which were fed through the theater's air-conditioning units. After just a couple of shows, the theater stank and Smellovision tanked.

> **"Who the hell wants to hear actors talk?"**
>
> —H. M. WARNER, FOUNDER OF WARNER BROTHERS, ON THE TOPIC OF ADDING SOUND TO MOVIES, IN 1927

Have a 16-year-old daughter who stays in her room crying all day

who stays out every night and you don't know where or with whom?

In 1998, 44% of Americans said that they would not want their 21-year-old daughter to intern in the Clinton White House.

Run one mile
with a cracked shinbone

OR

do 50 sit-ups on a hard floor
with a cracked tailbone?

While visiting Venezuela in 1958, Vice President Richard Nixon was spit upon by a protester. Secret Service agents quickly nabbed the perpetrator and held him while Nixon kicked him in the shins. Nixon later admitted in his book *Six Crises* that "nothing I did all day made me feel better."

GREAT RUNNERS DO THE MILE IN FOUR MINUTES (240 SECONDS).

GREAT SIT-UPPERS DO ONE PER SECOND.

For a living, clean silverware in your mouth

OR

clean golf balls in your mouth?

"ONE OF THE ADVANTAGES OF BOWLING OVER GOLF IS THAT YOU VERY SELDOM LOSE A BOWLING BALL."

—Don Carter, professional bowler

Former New Jersey Devils coach Tom McVie is the hit of any party because he can put three hockey pucks in his mouth at once.

As a woman, have the string of your tampon hang out of your bikini

OR

have a significant amount of visible pubic hair?

25 percent of women and 10 percent of men claim to shave all of their pubic hair regularly.

WHAT DO ELEPHANTS
USE FOR TAMPONS?
SHEEP.

As a man, lose two fingers off each hand

OR

lose ⅓ of your penis size?

Warning label on a Swedish chainsaw:

"Do not attempt to stop chain with your hands or genitals."

"God gave us a penis and a brain, but only enough blood to run one at a time."

—ROBIN WILLIAMS

Give up your three favorite hobbies

OR

lose your sex drive?

Should you lose your sex drive, don't worry. According to the World Health Organization, there are 100 million acts of sexual intercourse each day. So even with you out of the picture, there's still lots of sex driving going on.

A 97-year-old man goes into his doctor's office.

"Doc, I want my sex drive lowered."

"Sir," replied the doctor, "you're 97. Don't you think your 'sex drive' is all in your head?"

"You're damned right it is," replied the old man. "That's why I want it lowered!"

Immerse your naked body in a bathtub of cockroaches

OR

dive head first into a pool of chewing tobacco spit?

The cockroach—unlike the rat or mosquito—has never been linked with any epidemic of human disease.

THE WORLD RECORD FOR SPITTING A WATERMELON SEED IS ABOUT 70 FEET.

Eat a golfball-size
clump of wasabi
(green Japanese horseradish
eaten with sushi)

OR

a heaping tablespoon
of crushed red peppers
(the Italian kind eaten on pizza)?

A golf ball has
336 dimples.
Before 1850,
golf balls were
made of leather
and stuffed with
feathers.

Everything which inflames one's
appetite is likely to arouse the
other also. Pepper, mustard,
ketchup, and Worcestershire
sauce—shun them all. And even
salt, in any but the smallest
quantity, is objectionable; it is
such a goad toward carnalism
that the ancient fable depicted
Venus as born of the salt sea-wave.

—DIO LEWIS, M.D.
(AMERICAN PHYSICIAN, EDITOR, AND
LECTURER ON HYGIENE AND PHYSIOLOGY),
CHASTITY, OR, OUR SECRET SINS, 1874

Always be nauseated

always have a headache?

WHAT DO YOU THINK YOUR MOM AND DAD HAVE IN COMMON?

"Both don't want no more kids."
Lori, age 8

Be completely alone with nobody in the vicinity for one year

OR

never be alone for even one minute for one year?

A man joins a monastery that demands a vow of complete silence, except for every five years when he's permitted to say one thing to the head monk.

The man waits five years and then says, "The food here is not very good."

After another five years he says, "My bed's not comfortable."

And after another five years he says, "I'd like to leave."

"I think you should," replies the head monk. "You've done nothing but complain since you got here."

Have to eat the contents of a full vacuum-cleaner bag

OR

a pound of toe jam?

The 250,000 pores on the soles of your feet release about ¼ cup of sweat every day. Toe jam is made exclusively of dead skin cells, sweat, sock fabric, and dirt.

EVERY YEAR, THERE ARE ABOUT 15,000 VACUUM CLEANER—RELATED ACCIDENTS IN THE U.S.

MOST OF THE DUST IN YOUR HOUSE IS FLAKED-OFF SKIN.

Need to have sex once a day with a different person or die

OR

never have sex again?

Sally came home from a doctor's appointment in floods of tears. "Oh, Mom!" she sobbed, "I'm pregnant!"

"And who is the father?" demanded her mother.

The daughter lifted her tear-stained face and wailed, "How the hell would I know? You're the one who would never let me go steady."

ACCORDING TO THE *AMERICAN JOURNAL OF PUBLIC HEALTH*, THE AVERAGE AMERICAN WOMAN HAS INTERCOURSE 87 TIMES A YEAR (OR 1.7 TIMES A WEEK).

Place
a personal ad

OR

answer
a personal ad?

**THIRTY-FIVE PERCENT
OF THE PEOPLE WHO
USE PERSONAL ADS
FOR DATING ARE
ALREADY MARRIED.**

Be laughed at for something you are proud of

OR

not noticed at all?

DAN QUAYLE QUOTES

"It isn't pollution that's harming the environment. It's the impurities in our air and water that are doing it."

"One word sums up probably the responsibility of any vice president, and that one word is 'to be prepared.'"

"Hawaii has always been a very pivotal role in the Pacific. It is in the Pacific. It is a part of the United States that is an island that is right here."

"I love California. I practically grew up in Phoenix."

Perform a striptease for your teenaged children

OR

watch them do it?

In 1976, author Richard Wortly's *A Pictorial History of Strip Tease* was published. (Used copies now sell for about $150.)

In 1993, Patrick Angus's *Strip Show* was published. (One review noted that the book "captures a unique aspect of gay life that few have either experienced or are willing to admit.")

In 1999, Herbert I. Kavet's *How to Win at Strip Poker* was published. The book includes a deck of cards with pictures of women stripping *and* extra aces to make sure YOU win! (Atta boy, Herbert!)

Have to kill Winnie the Pooh

OR

Bambi?

A PENNSYLVANIA DILEMMA

In Pennsylvania, a bear-hunting license costs between twice and three times as much as a deer-hunting license (depending on whether you're a resident, or armed with a muzzle loader or a bow and arrow, or hunting doe or buck).

Why did Tigger look in the toilet?
He was trying to find poo.

Be forced to laugh in the most inappropriate situations

OR

have to say everything that is on your mind?

"SOMETIMES
I WISH I WERE
A LESBIAN . . .
DID I SAY THAT
OUT LOUD?"

—Matthew Perry as
Chandler on *Friends*

"The highlight of my
childhood was making
my brother laugh so
hard that food came
out of his nose."

—GARRISON KEILLOR

Find out that your neighbor installed a camera years ago that has taped everything that's gone on in your bedroom

OR

your bathroom?

"I caused my husband's heart attack. In the middle of love-making I took the paper bag off my head. He dropped the Polaroid and keeled over and so did the hooker. It would have taken me half an hour to untie myself and call the paramedics, but fortunately the Great Dane could dial."

—JOAN RIVERS

IN 1994, A MICHIGAN MAN, AFTER BEING CONVICTED OF SECRETLY VIDEOTAPING PEOPLE USING HIS BATHROOM, SERVED 75 DAYS IN JAIL.

When film director Billy Wilder went to Europe for the opening of *Some Like It Hot*, his wife asked him to send back Charvet ties for a friend and a bidet for herself. A couple of weeks later, Wilder cabled from France: "Charvet ties on way but impossible to obtain bidet. Suggest handstand in shower."

Always have a little black piece of spinach stuck between your teeth

OR

a little booger in your nose that moves when you breathe?

To clean the mucus out of their babies' noses, mothers in some Eskimo tribes suck the nose clean with their mouths and spit the mucus out on the ground. But nothing suggests these same mothers go around sucking small bits of spinach out of their babies' mouths.

IF YOU'RE A COW, THIS IS A NO-BRAINER. COWS HATE SPINACH.

Have an X-Acto knife blade shoved under your thumbnail

OR

have your nipple cut off with scissors?

To safely store an X-Acto knife (so that it doesn't get jammed under your thumbnail), cut a piece of dry sponge and bury the blade in it.

Most BDSM (bondage-and-discipline, sadism-and-masochism) Web sites suggest that when it comes to knives-and-nipples or scissors-and-nipples, this sort of play "should first be negotiated." DUH!

THE FOLLOWING IS ACTUALLY AN INSTRUCTION LABEL ON A KOREAN KITCHEN KNIFE:

WARNING: KEEP OUT OF CHILDREN.

Have everyone think your spouse is an idiot and a jerk

OR

that he or she is just really, really ugly?

"When turkeys mate they think of swans."
—JOHNNY CARSON

DIVORCE GRANTED! TO A LOS ANGELES WOMAN WHOSE HUSBAND MADE HER SCREW LIGHT BULBS IN AND OUT INSTEAD OF TURNING THEM ON AND OFF. HE DIDN'T WANT TO WEAR OUT THE SWITCHES.

Jell-O wrestle nude
in front of your family

OR

wear a diaper and
act like a baby in front of
someone you have a crush on?

**POCAHONTAS LIKED TO ENTERTAIN THE ENGLISH
COLONISTS BY PERFORMING CARTWHEELS IN THE
NUDE. JUST IMAGINE IF POCAHONTAS HAD BEEN
BORN LATER OR JELL-O HAD BEEN INVENTED EARLIER.**

On the first day of school, the first-grade teacher announced to her class
that they should put the baby talk of kindergarten behind them and start
using grown-up words. She then asked them to tell her what they did
during the summer.

The first little one said he went to see his nana.

The teacher said, "No, no, you went to see your grandmother. Use the
grown-up word."

The next little one said she went for a trip on a choo-choo.

The teacher again said, "No, no, you took a trip on a train. That's the
grown-up word."

Then the teacher asked the third little one what he did during the
summer. He proudly stated that he read a book. The teacher asked what
book he had read. He puffed out his chest and in a very adult way
replied, *"Winnie the Sh#t."*

Be caught doing something embarrassing in still photos

OR

on audiotape?

When George H. W. Bush served as the nation's vice president, only 56% of Americans recognized his photo; meanwhile, 93% recognized a photo of Mr. Clean.

> "I don't give a sh#t what happens. I want you all to stonewall it, let them plead the Fifth Amendment, cover up, or anything else. . . ."
>
> —PRESIDENT RICHARD NIXON, REFERRING TO THE WATERGATE INCIDENT ON AUDIOTAPE, TO THE NATION'S ATTORNEY GENERAL

Run across a field of 1,000 angry rattlesnakes

OR

three land mines?

Not too long ago, the Houston Zoo's curator admitted that the coral snakes on display are made of rubber "because the real ones keep dying."

A Southeastern Louisiana University biology professor put rubber reptiles "on or near roads" and watched how 22,000 drivers reacted to them. The results were as follows:

87% of the drivers tried to avoid the animals.

6% went out of their way to hit them. (One driver swerved to kill a snake, then U-turned and ran over it five more times.)

The remaining 7% must've driven by while the researchers were on a lunch break.

While rock climbing 500 feet up, lose one shoe

OR

both contact lenses?

DID YOU KNOW THAT IN THE ORIGINAL STORY OF CINDERELLA, ONE EVIL SISTER CUT HER OWN TOE OFF, AND THE OTHER HER OWN HEEL, TO CONVINCE THE PRINCE THAT THEIR FEET FIT IN THE SLIPPER? GROSS!

IT'S ESTIMATED THAT YOU'LL SPEND A YEAR OF YOUR LIFE LOOKING FOR MISPLACED OBJECTS.

Have the fire department extricate you from your own chimney after impersonating Santa Claus for your kids

OR

have your neighbors catch you trampling in their yard helping your kids TP (toilet paper) their house?

Santa needs all the help he can get . . .

There are an estimated 378 million Christian children in the world, according to Population Reference Bureau. At an average rate of 3.5 children per household, that's 91.8 million homes that Santa must deliver to each year.

On average, there are 333 squares of toilet paper on a roll. Assume one "tramp" per square and two tramps per second. Police are on patrol four minutes away. Knowing that the neighbors dialed 911 after your 54th tramp, how many more tramps are left until you're in handcuffs?

Answer: 32

Have your country engage in a policy of isolationism

OR

a policy of overzealous world protectionism?

If you have money in the bank, in your wallet, and spare change in a dish someplace, you are among the top 8% of the world's wealthy.

IF YOU HAVE FOOD IN THE REFRIGERATOR, CLOTHES ON YOUR BACK, A ROOF OVERHEAD, AND A PLACE TO SLEEP, YOU ARE RICHER THAN 75% OF THE PEOPLE IN THE WORLD.

Be separated from your family (parents, siblings, children) and never see them again

OR

live with them for the rest of your life in a two-bedroom house?

Joined to one another at the chest, Siamese twins Chang and Eng fathered 21 children. Eng was a teetotaler, but Chang loved his liquor. Literally attached face-to-face, often half-drunk, they argued endlessly about the booze. This went on for 59 years (1811–1870).

"HI, MY NAME IS GEORGE, I'M UNEMPLOYED AND I LIVE WITH MY PARENTS."

—Jason Alexander as George Costanza on *Seinfeld*

In golf, get a hole in one that makes the *Guinness Book of Records,* but accidentally throw your club on the follow-through and put a bystander in the hospital for a week

make the hole in one and have no witness?

Well, whatever you do, be sure to write to the *Guinness Book of Records,* tell them exactly which record you think you broke, and request the guidelines for that record. As follows:

The Guinness Book of Records
Six Landmark Square
Stamford, CT 06901-2704

Meanwhile, about 30,000 golfers hit holes in one every year. The odds against hitting one are pretty high: 10,738 to 1.

Discover that space aliens are superior to ourselves

OR

inferior?

LEGALLY, YOU OWN ANY METEORITE
THAT FALLS ON YOUR LAND.
THE LAW'S NOT SO CLEAR ABOUT
ANY SPACE ALIEN THAT FALLS
ON YOUR LAND, NO MATTER
HOW BRIGHT HE/SHE/IT MAY BE.

Meanwhile, as of
October 31, 2000, if things
go according to NASA's plans,
there will never be another day
without earthlings in space.

Eat
15 feet of aluminum foil

OR

swallow
6 steel guitar strings?

TOP 2 SWALLOWERS!!

A 24-year-old American woman gulped down
a five-inch hinge bolt from her hospital door.
It passed through the curve of the duodenum
and the intestinal tract, only to break a
bedpan when she successfully passed it.

Babe Ruth once downed 12 hot dogs between
games of a doubleheader.

Have to hold a one-inch roach
in your mouth, unharmed,
for five minutes

OR

have to lie motionless on
a termite nest for ten minutes?

First things first:

1. Is this a "cock" roach or a "joint" roach?
2. Is a rock 'n' roll band involved?
3. Do you like cats?
4. How do you feel about farting?

1. If it's a "joint" roach, this is a no-brainer.
2. Termites chew at twice their usual speed when listening to rock music.
3. A cockroach spends more time cleaning itself than a cat does.
4. Termites have microcreatures in their stomachs to help them digest wood. Because these little stomach creatures produce a lot of methane, termites fart like crazy.

Marry a person who loves you but whom you will never love

OR

marry someone you love but who will never love you?

THE WIT AND WISDOM OF MARRIAGE AND LOVE
(the miniedition)

"There is so little difference between husbands,
you might as well keep the first."
—ADELA ROGERS ST. JOHNS

"Marriage is really tough because you have to
deal with feelings and lawyers."
—RICHARD PRYOR

"Nothing anybody tells you about marriage helps."
—MAX SIEGEL

Lose your mate to the same sex as yourself

OR

to the opposite sex?

OR to a flagpole?
Remember Frank Perkins, the guy who lost the 400-day world flagpole-sitting record because he caught the flu? Sometime during those 399 ⅓ days, his sponsor had gone bust, his phone and electricity had been cut off, and his girlfriend had left him.

HOW WOULD YOU MAKE A MARRIAGE WORK?

"Tell your wife that she looks pretty even if she looks like a truck."
Ricky, age 10

Suck clean
an unknown person's
set of dentures

OR

eat popcorn
that has been blown out
of an elephant's trunk?

Elephants drink 50 gallons of water a day, eat 250 pounds of plants, like to chew tobacco, love to drink beer, and are the only animals, other than man, that can be taught to stand on their heads.

THE AVERAGE HUMAN MOUTH PRODUCES A QUART OF SALIVA EVERY DAY.

Have questionable integrity

OR

no sense of humor?

"YOU CAN PRETEND TO BE SERIOUS;
YOU CAN'T PRETEND TO BE WITTY."
—Sacha Guitry

"HONESTY IS THE BEST POLICY AND
SPINACH IS THE BEST VEGETABLE."
—Popeye

"YOU GROW UP THE DAY YOU HAVE
THE FIRST GREAT LAUGH—AT YOURSELF."
—Ethel Barrymore

"DYING IS EASY. COMEDY IS DIFFICULT."
—Edmund Gwenn, actor, on his deathbed

Lick the floor underneath a refrigerator

OR

the underside of a toilet rim?

THE JULY 2000 ISSUE OF THE *JOURNAL OF APPLIED MICROBIOLOGY* REPORTED THAT GERMS COULD CONTINUE TO GROW INSIDE A TOILET BOWL FOR AS LONG AS FOUR WEEKS.

There is more contamination in the average kitchen than in the average bathroom. Sixty percent more of it is found in kitchen sponges than in bathrooms; fifty percent more in kitchen sinks (researchers found more fecal matter in kitchen sinks than in toilet bowls); and twenty-five percent more on countertops.

When faced with an attacking grizzly bear, be armed with a guitar made of solid maple

OR

with a saxophone?

If several people meet up with a grizzly bear, they should stay calm and link arms with each other. Confronted with a larger creature, the bear is likely to retreat. Supposedly.

Just like presidents who play the saxophone, grizzly bears are wildly promiscuous. (What good this does when faced with fighting off a grizzly bear we have no idea. But the notion of putting "saxophone," "grizzly bears," and "wildly promiscuous" into a factually correct 12-word sentence was too rare an opportunity to pass up.)

As a writer, lose your life's work because your computer crashed

have someone steal your idea and make a fortune?

On November 28, 1922, the absolutely only copies—including carbons—of many of Hemingway's short stories were stolen from his luggage at the Gare de Lyon.

"WHAT DO PEOPLE MEAN WHEN THEY SAY 'THE COMPUTER WENT DOWN ON ME'?"
—Marilyn Pittman

Have an eyelash permanently affixed to your eyeball

OR

a prickly burr permanently poking into your heel?

RESEARCHERS SAY IT'S IMPOSSIBLE TO SNEEZE WITH YOUR EYES OPEN.

In 1804, United States vice president Aaron Burr shot American statesman Alexander Hamilton in the groin during their famous duel. Talk about a prickly Burr. . . .

Have a baby
that cries twice as loud and
often as other babies

OR

one that goes to the bathroom
twice as often
but is very quiet and
well behaved?

In the 1980s, Frenchwomen Dominique
Peignoux, Yvette Guys, and Françoise
Dekan marketed a musical napkin that
was placed inside a baby's diaper and
played "When the Saints Go Marching
In" as soon as it became wet.

Be sterile

OR

never be able to use birth control?

WHAT IS THE BEST BIRTH CONTROL FOR SENIOR CITIZENS? *NUDITY!*

CONDOMS ARE THE MOST COMMON FORM OF BIRTH CONTROL IN JAPAN. THE BIRTH CONTROL PILL WAS NOT WIDELY AVAILABLE THERE UNTIL 1999.

Sleep in a human-size nest in a tree

in a burrow underground?

Five percent of adults sleepwalk.

Underground is the only word in the English language that begins and ends with the letters U-N-D. (Discovered by some unemployed writer spending too much time in his underground burrow. Had the guy been a bookkeeper instead, he might have figured out that his profession is the only word in the English language with three consecutive double letters.)

Have a little red blinking light in the lower corner of your vision

OR

have a constant pinging in your ear?

The safer choice here is probably the pinging. Supposedly, red rooms cause people to act with reckless abandon. That's why so many casinos are decorated in red. Have that red blinking light in the lower corner of your vision and surely your home, car, 401K, children—everything!—will have been left on the craps table by noon.

Constant pinging, on the other hand, will just drive you nuts.

Only be able to spend a total of three months a year with your significant other

OR

be handcuffed together for life?

Maybe being handcuffed to *this* woman would be OK:

A woman lawyer defending a man accused of burglary tried a creative defense: "My client merely inserted his arm into the window and removed a few trifling articles. His arm is not himself, and I fail to see how you can punish the whole individual for an offense committed by his limb."

"Well put," the judge replied. "Using your logic, I sentence the defendant's arm to one year's imprisonment. He can accompany it or not, as he chooses."

The defendant smiled. With his lawyer's assistance he detached his artificial limb, laid it on the bench, and walked out.

HOW CAN A STRANGER TELL IF TWO PEOPLE ARE MARRIED?

"Married people usually look happy to talk to other people." *Eddie, age 6*

"You might have to guess, based on whether they seem to be yelling at the same kids." *Derrick, age 8*

Have a mouse run up your pants leg

OR

a wasp get caught inside your shirt?

ONLY FEMALE WASPS CAN STING, BUT THEY ARE ABLE TO STING REPEATEDLY.

AT NIGHT, A HUNGRY OWL CAN HEAR THE MOVEMENTS OF A LITTLE MOUSE RUNNING AROUND UNDER THE SNOW. OR UP YOUR PANTS LEG.

Stick your hand into a box filled with fire ants

into a box with unknown contents?

According to statistical research, more surgical repairs are performed on the hand than on any other part of the body. Here's your chance to be a *handy* statistic!

Carry a 70-pound backpack for ten miles

OR

a 30-pound briefcase for ten miles?

Do you weigh about 500 pounds? If so, go with the 70-pound backpack.

Those in the know say that children should carry no more than 15% of their body weight on their backs.* Fifteen percent of 500 pounds is 75 pounds. So you can handle the 70 pounds, even for ten miles (notice that there's no time limit).

Atta boy, fatso!

*But here's the problem: with the average textbook weighing five or six pounds, most schoolchildren are exceeding this limit by two or three times over.

After having just run ten miles as fast as you can, find out you have to run three more miles

OR

that you have to walk ten more miles?

Sarah Covington-Fulcher did a run of 11,134 miles around the United States.

George Meegan walked the 19,109 miles from the southern tip of South America to Prudhoe Bay in northern Alaska.

"The trouble with jogging is that by the time you realize you're not in shape for it, it's too far to walk back."

—FRANKLIN JONES

Have to try to kill three wild rattlesnakes while you are armed with only a bowling ball

OR

sit still while thousands of honeybees form a beard on your face?

FIFTEEN PERCENT OF RATTLESNAKE BITES COME FROM SNAKES THAT HAVE BEEN DEAD AT LEAST SEVERAL MINUTES. RATTLESNAKE BITING IS A REFLEX ACTION THAT TAKES A WHILE TO SHUT DOWN.

MEANWHILE, BEES—LIKE DOGS—SMELL FEAR.

Tell your wife at a fashion show
what a fat pig she is
(with no explanation)

OR

boo your son at his school play
during his performance
(with no explanation)?

A PIG JOKE

Farmer Smith got out of his car and while heading for his friend's door, noticed a pig with a wooden leg. His curiosity roused, he asked, "Fred, how'd that pig get him a wooden leg?"

"Well, Zeb, that's a mighty special pig! A while back a wild boar attacked me while I was walking in the woods. That pig there came a-runnin', went after that boar, and chased him away. Saved my life!"

"And the boar tore up his leg?"

"No, he was fine after that. But a bit later we had that fire. Started in the shed up against the barn. Well, that ole pig started squealin' like he was stuck, woke us up, and 'fore we got out here, the dern thing had herded the other animals out of the barn and saved 'em all!"

"So that's when he hurt his leg?"

"No, Zeb. He was a might winded, though. When my tractor hit a rock and rolled down the hill into the pond I was knocked clean out. When I came to, that pig had dove into the pond and dragged me out 'fore I drownded. Sure did save my life."

"And that was when he hurt his leg?"

"Oh no, he was fine. Cleaned him up, too."

"OK, Fred. So just tell me. How did he get the wooden leg?"

"Well," the farmer says, "a pig like that you don't want to eat all at once."

Always lose

OR

never play?

IN A GAME OF INTERCOLLEGIATE
FOOTBALL PLAYED ON OCTOBER 8, 1916,
GEORGIA TECH BEAT CUMBERLAND
UNIVERSITY 222 TO 0.

NO ONE EVER SAYS
"IT'S ONLY A GAME"
WHEN THEIR TEAM
IS WINNING.

SGT. HULKA: You know
something, soldier. . . .
I've noticed you're
always last.

WINGER (Bill Murray):
I'm pacing myself,
Sergeant.

—FROM *STRIPES*

Be able to walk on water forever

OR

fly for three hours on three different occasions in your life?

Crouching Tiger, Hidden Dragon has caused quite a few injuries as children attempt to fly across rooftops like the film's actors.

A HAIKU BY URKOV

Buoyancy by choice
Would send several scholars
To their therapists

—Michael Urkov, Redding, CA

With no experience whatsoever and with your life depending on a finish in the top half of the field, have to be a jockey in the Kentucky Derby

OR

a driver in the Indy 500?

"ALL I HAD TO DO WAS
KEEP TURNING LEFT."

—George Robson,
after winning the Indy 500

Have to steal from a blind man

`OR`

a Girl Scout?

"It is a mean thief or a successful author that plunders the dead."

—AUSTIN O'MALLEY
(1858–1932)

BLINKIES IS WHAT POLICE CALL BEGGARS WHO PRETEND TO BE BLIND.

Be offensive

OR

incredibly passive?

Q. HOW MANY MEN DOES IT TAKE TO OPEN
A CAN OF BEER?

A. NONE. IT SHOULD BE OPEN BY THE TIME
SHE BRINGS IT TO THE COUCH.

Live in a world where you needed a quarter to get into every bathroom (including the one in your home)

 OR

where every bathroom only had one square of tissue?

A quarter or free, one square of tissue or a million, the first toilet stall in a public bathroom is usually the cleanest. Slobs, in need of privacy to do their slobbiness, shy away from it.

Wear a motorcycle helmet to bed every night

always sleep with shoes and jeans on?

HERE WE ARE, AT THE VERY LAST
QUESTION. AND EACH ONE HAS
CONTAINED THE LETTER "E"
(AND "O" AND "R").
YET ERNEST VINCENT WRIGHT
WAS ABLE TO WRITE *GADSBY*,
A 50,000-WORD NOVEL,
WITHOUT EVER USING THE LETTER "E."